International FOLK DANCE *at a glance*

Second Edition

CECILE GILBERT

Ball State University
Indiana

Burgess Publishing Company
Minneapolis, Minnesota 55435

Editorial Consultants:

Eloise M. Jaeger
Robert D. Clayton

Copyright © 1974, 1969 by Burgess Publishing Company
Printed in the United States of America
Library of Congress Card Number 73-90229
SBN 8087-0727-2

2 3 4 5 6 7 8 9 0

Front cover photos: Top—Supplied by VILTIS Folk Dance Magazine, P.O. Box 1226, Denver, Colorado, 80201; bottom left—Supplied by The Folk Dance Federation of California North, Inc.; bottom right—Courtesy of Robert J. Decker, Muskingum College, New Concord, Ohio.

Back cover: Top left and top right—Supplied by VILTIS Folk Dance Magazine; middle—By Nelson R. Smith. Supplied by VILTIS Folk Dance Magazine; bottom—By Harry L. Bloom. Supplied by The Folk Dance Federation of California North, Inc.

PREFACE

This book is intended for all people who enjoy folk dancing!

It is intended for people who are learning to folk dance as well as for those who are teaching. It is intended for people who are interested in folk dance as a school or as a recreational activity. It is for the beginner as well as for the experienced dancer.

Folk dancing has become a very popular recreational activity. Hundreds of groups are dancing. There are workshops and camps specializing in folk dancing in almost every part of the country. Those who are interested keep adding more and more dances to their repertoire.

It is impossible to retain a dance unless it is danced! An experienced dancer may have known and danced hundreds of dances; but unless he is reminded about which foot starts, what formation is used, in what direction is the first movement, what is the sequence of main parts of the dance, it is difficult for him to bring to mind any one particular dance. And that is exactly what this book does!

Although the main purpose of this book is to help the reader to recall instantly a dance he had once known, there are other ways in which this book may prove to be useful.

One can learn a new dance by following the directions, arrows and counts as given here. One can't go wrong if the directions and the arrows are followed carefully. Because many of the dances in this collection are easy non-partner dances, they should be very usable in a recreation situation.

Because this book came into existence as a textbook for folk dance classes for the general college student, it must contain dances which cover a wide range of degree of difficulty. The dances range from the very simple ones such as the Hora, Troika, and Ve David which are suitable for the first days of the beginning class to the very exciting dances such as the Godečki Čačak and the Haroa Haktana which are suitable for the intermediate and advanced classes.

In recent years a wealth of material has been published on the subject of folk dancing. For those who are interested, a bibliography of excellent folk dance books is included in the appendix.

No attempt has been made to make a complete listing of records for each dance. Students often ask where they can buy records. For them, sources are listed in the appendix.

The dances which are included were chosen because they are fun to do and because they provide a variety of basic steps, formations, and nationalities, including dances from Africa which have not been published previously. It is the author's hope that the reader will find them enjoyable.

ACKNOWLEDGMENTS

It would be impossible to thank all of the people who contributed to this book because many of them are unknown to the author. Therefore, the writer takes this opportunity to extend grateful acknowledgments to all those anonymous persons who did research, introduced dances, directed and taught at workshops, and in various other ways encouraged the growth of folk dancing.

In addition, the writer wishes to express special thanks to the following people:

To Ruth E. Andrews, Head of the Women's Physical Education Department, Ball State University, Muncie, Indiana for her patience, interest, and encouragement;

To Fred Berk, Mary Ann Herman, and Ralph Page who are outstanding among the many fine teachers with whom the writer was privileged to study;

To her colleagues, Adelaide Cole, Yaakov Eden, Rosemary Fisher, Gale Gehlsen, Eileen Keener, Charlotte Korsgaard, Diane Kourim, Nancy Linson, Coranell Rossow, and Sandra Stultz who so graciously tested the materials with their students;

To Yoav Ashriel, V. F. Beliajus, Mary and Fred Collette, Richard Crum, Andor Czompo, Alura F. de Angeles, Ada Dziewanowska, Paul and Gretal Dunsing, Jane Farwell, Mary and Jan Garrity, Michael Herman, Shalom Hermon, Mary Joyce, Anatol Joukowsky, Odinga Lumumba, Annette Macdonald, and Millie von Konsky for so generously giving permission to use their dances;

To Larry Simmons for his delightful drawings;

And lastly, to the author's many students who have provided inspiration through their wonderful enthusiasm and love for folk dancing.

January 1974
Cecile Gilbert

CONTENTS

INTRODUCTION TO FOLK DANCE

In a book which deals mainly with dance notations there is not enough room for a long dissertation on the history of folk dancing. Other authors have written complete volumes on the subject, but a few words about the background of folk dancing are in order here.

Surely every thinking person must realize that folk dance (the dance of the people) did not spring full-blown into existence. As is true of any other folk art, the roots of folk dance are buried deep in antiquity. Dance, as a rhythmical form of movement, was one of the earliest forms of communication and, as a form of communication, it became part of everyday life activities; it reinforced important occasions; it was an integral component of religious rituals.

Today we folk dance mainly because it is such a delight to move rhythmically with others. Folk dance is a living activity and, as a living activity, it is constantly changing. Before the advent of written descriptions of dances, dances were handed down from one generation to the next. If a foot pattern were too difficult it was changed. If the new generation wanted to add something to make the dance livelier it did so. Some dances were kept exactly the same with absolutely no change although the original purposes of the dances were long ago forgotten.

For folk dance enthusiasts there is a constant search for answers. For example:

Why do the Yugoslavs dance flat footed? Is it because they live in a mountainous area and find walking easier if done on a flat foot?

Why is Greek dancing so deliciously satisfying and relaxing in an understated manner? Is it because of the Golden Age of Greece when everything was so perfect?

Why is Spanish dancing so fiery in spots and so languid in others? Is it because the temperament of the people is so unpredictable?

Why is Israeli dancing so exciting and so vigorous? Is it because Israel is a young country and the people, especially the native born Sabras, are so young and vigorous?

Why is the circle formation the most common folk dance formation? Is it because originally the people joined hands and moved around a magic object or a tree god?

Why did Contra dances become so popular? Was it because the early builders made a roof of tree trunks and the length of the tree determined the width of the room, giving the people long narrow rooms?

Why do the Russian men do the show-off squat steps whereas the women do not? Is it because the undergarments of the women would not allow this type of movement?

Why have the non-partner dances become the most popular type of dances within the last ten years? Is it because the young people in our society do not want to take the responsibility of choosing a partner, thereby implying an accountability to that person?

Why is there a decline in the popularity of couple dances? Is it because the closed social dance position was a socially acceptable way to touch and feel and hold a loved one and now in our modern society when young people are so bold about fondling each other in public there is no longer the need for subterfuge?

So many different things may influence the styling of a country's dance—the climate, the topography, the history, the clothing, the religion, the footwear, the temperament. The questions could go on and on and the search for answers is fascinating and never-ending.

Folk dance is a dynamic art form, ever changing.

VALUES OF FOLK DANCE

Folk dancing meets the objectives of physical education better than any other one activity in the field. Besides being a joyous activity in its own right, it promotes physical fitness through vigorous sustained activity; it develops body balance, poise, and neuromuscular coordination; it helps people to relate to people—to see our differences and similarities through dance. Most important is the fact that it is a wholesome type of activity for co-ed groups which often becomes a life time recreational activity.

COURTESIES OF FOLK DANCE

Remember the Golden Rule and practice it.
When joining a kolo line, join at the tail end.
Try not to form cliques—dance with everyone.
Help those who are weaker than you; learn from those who are better than you.
There are endless variations of dances. Therefore when you are a guest, dance the way the host group dances. When others come to dance with your group, they should dance your way.
There is no right or wrong to dance a dance. People dance the same dance in different ways simply because they come from "different villages."

SYMBOLS

R	Right		M	Man
L	Left		W	Woman
;	A semicolon denotes the end of a measure.			

↑	Forward		↖	Diagonally forward to left
↓	Backward		↗	Diagonally forward to right
→	To the right		↘	Diagonally backward to right
←	To the left		↙	Diagonally backward to left
⤳	Turning to right		⤳	Turning to left

⇡   Broken arrow means the action is done in the direction in which the arrow points but there is no weight on the foot that does the action.

↑   Unbroken arrow (unless other directions are given) means to <u>STEP</u> in the direction in which the arrow points.

Any action which is performed by the L foot and moves to the R (as $\vec{L}$ or $\overset{\nearrow}{L}$ or $\overset{\searrow}{L}$) crosses the center line of the body.

Any action which is performed by the R foot and moves to the L (as $\overset{\leftarrow}{R}$ or $\overset{\nwarrow}{R}$ or $\overset{\swarrow}{R}$) crosses the center line of the body.

CW	Clockwise
CCW	Counterclockwise
(R)	L or R inside parentheses means there is no weight on that foot.
(4)	A number inside parentheses means there is no action on that count.
LOD	Line of direction. Usually counterclockwise.
RLOD	Reverse line of direction.
Ptnr	Partner
Wt	Weight
Pl	In place is beside the supporting foot.

When numbers follow an action word, that same action should be repeated for each number.
"RUN TWO THREE FOUR" means four runs.

For each dance:

1. Say the capitalized words.
2. Do what you say
3. In the direction of the arrow
4. With the indicated foot.

1

BASIC MOVEMENTS

Most dances use fundamental movements which involve only one contact with the floor or traditional dance steps which are combinations of the fundamental movements put to various rhythms.

> **For each dance:**
>
> 1. Say the capitalized words.
> 2. Do what you say
> 3. In the direction of the arrow
> 4. With the indicated foot.

FUNDAMENTAL MOVEMENTS — ONE ACTION

WALK
or
STEP

One action — start with weight on one foot; change weight from one foot to the other
Any direction
Either foot

RUN

One action — start with weight on one foot; spring into the air; land on the other foot
Any Direction
Both feet are momentarily off the floor during the change of weight

LEAP

Same as run but bigger
Stronger

HOP

One action
Either foot
Start with weight on one foot
Spring into air
Land on the same foot

JUMP

One action — start with weight on both feet
Spring into the air
Land on both feet

JEAP*

Start with weight on both feet (as beginning of JUMP)
Spring into air
Land on one foot (as end of LEAP)

LUMP*

Start with weight on one foot (as beginning of LEAP)
Spring into air
Land on both feet (as end of JUMP)

*These beautifully descriptive words were coined by Shirley Wimmer, Director, School of Dance, Ohio University, Athens, Ohio, to clarify the variations of the JUMP.

BASIC MOVEMENTS — TWO OR MORE ACTIONS

STEP-HOP

One
Step-hop

1	2
STEP	HOP
↑	
L	L

Two actions
Two counts, even time
May start on either foot
May move in any direction
In a series, start the next step-hop on the
    other foot
Often used in combination with the schottische
    as a unit of two schottische and four
    step-hops.

Four
Step-hops

1	2	3	4		1	2	3	4
STEP	HOP	STEP	HOP;		STEP	HOP	STEP	HOP;
↑		↑			↑		↑	
L	L	R	R		L	L	R	R

SCHOTTISCHE

1	2	3	4
STEP	STEP	STEP	HOP
↑	↑	↑	
L	R	L	L

Four actions, four counts, even time
May start on either foot
May move in any direction
In a series, start the next schottische on the
    other foot.

MAZURKA

1	2	3
STEP	CLOSE	HOP
↖		
L	R	R

Three actions
Three counts, even time
Start with either foot
In a series, start every mazurka with the <u>same</u>
    foot
(While hopping, swing back of L heel across in
    front of R shinbone)

TWO-STEP

Fast Two-step

1	&	2
STEP	CLOSE	STEP
↑		↑
L	R	L

Three actions
Two counts
Uneven time (quick-quick-slow)
May start on either foot
May move in any direction
In a series, start the next two-step on the
    other foot

Slow Two-step

1	2	3	(4)
STEP	CLOSE	STEP	- - - - - -
↑		↑	
L	R	L	

Three actions
Four counts
Uneven time (quick-quick-slow)
May start on either foot
May move in any direction
In a series, start the next two-step on the
    other foot

POLKA

ah	1	&	2
HOP	STEP	CLOSE	STEP
	↑		↑
R	L	R	L

Four actions
Two counts
Uneven time
May start on either foot
May move in any direction
In a series, start the next polka on the other foot
Learn the fast two-step first, then do a little hop in front of each two-step

POLKA RIGHT TURN

ah	1	&	2
HOP	STEP	CLOSE	STEP
↘	←		↑
R	L	R	L

Go sideways on the "step-close-step" and turn a half turn to your right (clockwise on the "hop")
Move counterclockwise around the room

YEMENITE

Yemenite Right

1	2	3	(4)
STEP	CLOSE	CROSS	———
→		↖	
R	L	R	

Three actions
Four counts
Uneven time
May use either foot
May start in any direction
In a series, start the next Yemenite with the other foot

Yemenite Left

1	2	3	(4)
STEP	CLOSE	CROSS	———
←		↗	
L	R	L	

First action — step in a direction
Second action — close (or may be other side)
Third action — step in direction which is opposite from first action but use the first foot

TCHERKESSIA

(Pronounced Chair-keh-sée-yah)

1	2	3	4
FORWARD	BACK	BEHIND	STEP
↑	↓	↓	↑
R	L	R	L

Four actions
Four counts
Even time
In a series, start the next Tcherkessia on the same foot as the first one

MAYIM

1	2	3	4
FRONT	SIDE	BEHIND	LEAP
↙	←	↙	←
R	L	R	L

Four actions
Four counts
Even time
In a series, start the next Mayim on the same foot as the first one
Similar to TCHERKESSIA but moving left
Teach Tcherkessia first

DOUBLE TCHERKESSIA

Six actions
Six counts
Even time

1	2	3	4	5	6
CROSS	BACK	STEP	CROSS	BACK	STEP
		(beside L)			(beside R)
↖	↘		↗	↙	
R	L	R	L	R	L

WALTZ

Forward Waltz

1	2	3
STEP	SIDE	CLOSE
↑	→	
L	R	L

Three actions
Three counts
Even time
May start on either foot
May move in any direction
In a series, start the next waltz on the other foot

Backward Waltz

1	2	3
STEP	SIDE	CLOSE
↓	→	
L	R	L

Waltz Walk

1	2	3
STEP	STEP	STEP
↑	↑	↑
L	R	L

Left Forward Box Waltz (The left foot starts the forward waltz.)

1	2	3	1	2	3
STEP	SIDE	CLOSE;	BACK	SIDE	CLOSE;
↑	→		↓	←	
L	R	L	R	L	R

Right Forward Box Waltz (The right foot starts the forward waltz.)

1	2	3	1	2	3
STEP	SIDE	CLOSE;	BACK	SIDE	CLOSE;
↓	→		↑	←	
L	R	L	R	L	R

GERMAN WALTZ (Notice the " close" is on count "2.")

1	2	3
STEP	CLOSE	STEP
↑		↑
L	R	L

WALTZ BALANCE

One waltz balance takes one measure of waltz music (3 counts).
The important part is to step firmly forward or backward on count "one."
The actions of counts "two" and "three" are used mainly to keep time in place.
The waltz balance may be started on either foot.
May move in any direction.
In a series of waltz balances, start the next waltz balance on the other foot and usually in the other direction.

Basic Movements 5

A Waltz Balance forward and a Waltz Balance backward.

1	2	3	1	2	3
FRONT	UP	DOWN;	BACK	UP	DOWN;
	(close R to L)	(lower heels)		(close L to R)	(lower heels)
	(rise on toes)			(rise on toes)	
↑			↓		
L	both	both	R	both	both

Modified Waltz Balance forward and backward

1	2	3	1	2	3
FRONT	STEP	STEP;	BACK	STEP	STEP;
↑	(beside L)	(beside R)	↓	(beside R)	(beside L)
L	R	L	R	L	R

TURNING WALTZ

Good dancers should be able to do the waltz turn to the left (counterclockwise body turn) or to the right (clockwise body turn).

Almost all folk dances use the clockwise body turn while progressing counterclockwise around the room. It takes two measures of waltz music to complete one turn.

Clockwise Waltz Turn

Count 1 — Step into the line of direction with either
 a. the back of the LEFT HEEL leading, or
 b. the front of the RIGHT TOE leading.

Count 2, 3 — Turn half around to your right (clockwise) with two steps. Be sure you take a step on each count. Make the steps very small. Stay in one spot, but turn hard.

Continue as above — If the left foot is free, step backward into the line of direction. If the right foot is free, step forward into the line of direction.

Man's part of Clockwise Waltz Turn

1	2	3	1	2	3
BACK	TURN	TURN;	FORWARD	TURN	TURN;
↙	↷	↷	↑	↷	↷
L	R	L	R	L	R

Woman's part of Clockwise Waltz Turn

1	2	3	1	2	3
FRONT	TURN	TURN;	BACK	TURN	TURN;
↑	↷	↷	↓	↷	↷
R	L	R	L	R	L

Suggestions for improving the clockwise waltz turn.

1. It helps if the man is facing the closest wall before he starts the waltz turn.
2. When the right foot steps forward (for man or woman), it should go inside between partner's two feet. Dovetail the feet.
3. Remember to step forward with the right foot in the line of direction or backward with the left foot in the line of direction on count "one."
4. Turn hard on counts "two" and "three," but don't try to cover much distance.

PAS DE BAS
or
PAS DE BASQUE

(Pronounced Pah-dee-bah)

2/4 or 4/4	1	&	2
	LEAP –	STEP –	STEP
	→	↗	↙
	R –	L –	R

or

3/4	1	2	3
	LEAP	STEP	STEP
	→	↗	↙
	R	L	R

Three actions
Two counts in 2/4 or 4/4
   (or three counts in 3/4)
Uneven time in 2/4 or 4/4
   (or even time in 3/4)
In a series, start the next pas de bas on the other foot.

(quick, quick, slow)

Similar to a FAST TWO-STEP which
   is danced on one spot.

(slow, slow, slow)

POSITIONS

COUPLE POSITION

Side by side.

Woman on right of man.

Hold inside hand.

His hand underneath.

CLOSED SOCIAL DANCE POSITION

Face partner squarely.

His R hand flat and firm in middle of her back.

His R elbow points sideward — not down. This forms a shelf for the woman's L arm.

Straight line from his fingertips to elbow of R arm.

Her L hand is placed firmly on his R shoulder.

Her lower arm should touch his upper arm. The contact is helpful to the man in leading.

His L hand holds her R hand in easy relaxed manner.

CONVERSATION POSITION

Side by side.

Woman on right.

Man's R hand in middle of woman's back (as in closed position).

Woman's L hand on his shoulder (as in closed position).

OPEN POSITION

Same as conversation position except that man's L hand holds woman's R hand.

Both face line of direction.

PROMENADE POSITION

Side by side.

Woman on R.

L hand to L hand.

R hand to R hand above left.

(Similar to skating position except that in skating position the R hand is underneath to help support partner.)

VARSOVIENNE POSITION

Side by side.

Woman on R.

L hand to L hand in front.

R hand to R hand beside woman's R shoulder. His R elbow is behind woman's back.

SHOULDER-WAIST POSITION

Face partner squarely.

Man's hands at woman's waist.

Woman's hands on his shoulders.

BUTTERFLY POSITION

Face partner squarely.

Both hands joined.

Arms outstretched shoulder height.

Arms are easy and relaxed.

TEACHING SUGGESTIONS

Get into it quickly — don't talk them to death.

Stand where <u>all</u> can see you and hear you (<u>not</u> in the <u>middle</u> of the circle).

Four main points to follow:

1. **PREPARE THEM**

   Work on basics ahead of time.
   Motivate them by giving background of the dance or the people.

2. **SHOW THEM** (unless the dance looks more difficult than it is)

   Demonstrate the complete dance to music.
   Some students will catch on just from seeing it performed.
   All students will know what they are heading toward.

3. **TEACH THEM**

   Break it down into small units.
   Re-demonstrate each unit.
   Verbalize it in slow motion.
   Drill them on the more difficult parts.
   Cue them when you put it together.

4. **CORRECT THEM**

   Find their errors and help them change to the right way.
   Commend them when they are doing well.

ADDITIONAL AIDS

<u>Verbalize</u> — This means (a) to say <u>one</u> descriptive word for each action. (b) These words must be said in the <u>correct</u> <u>rhythm</u> of the action.

This is one of the best teaching techniques. If the class verbalizes along with the teacher it is even more helpful because it helps them remember the actions.

<u>Reminders</u> or cues — These are words that are given <u>ahead</u> of the next action. The words should be informational to help the student know what's coming next. The reminders may tell the next direction or the next formation or the next action.

Verbalizing is done <u>while</u> you are teaching.

Reminders are given <u>after</u> the dance has been taught but before the class is sure of the sequence.

<u>Starting Signals</u> should consist of two parts, such as "Ready, <u>and</u>" or "Ready, <u>go</u>" or "Now, <u>begin</u>."

Remember — The teacher's enthusiasm is the most important teaching technique.

ALEXANDROVSKA

Russian couple dance

Pronounced Alex-an-dróff-skah

This is a ballroom type of dance which is very smooth and quite elegant. It is performed with great dignity. Probably named in honor of Czar Alexander, it was popular at the end of the 1800s and during the early 1900s. Many variations are danced in the United States; in the eastern part of our country it is called Alexandrovsky.

Records: Folk Dancer MH 1057
Folkraft 1107

Formation: Double circle. Face partner.

Man's back to center.

Hold two hands shoulder height (butterfly position).

Line of direction (LOD) is counterclockwise (CCW).

Directions are for man. Woman uses other foot.

Free foot — Man's L, woman's R.

Music 3/4

Measures
1-4   Introduction

(On swing through, hold one hand — man's R, woman's L.) (You are now back to back — move CCW in LOD.)

		1	2	3	1	2	3
1-2		SIDE	——	CLOSE;	SIDE	SWING	THRU;
		←			←		←--
		L		R	L	(R)	
						(turn your back to partner)	

A
Swing
Thru

(Back to partner)

		1	2	3	1	2	3
3-4		SIDE	——	CLOSE;	SIDE	TOUCH	——;
		→			→	(beside R)	
		R		L	R	(L)	

Continue holding one hand — man's <u>R</u> and woman's <u>L</u> — until you dance "B."

| 5-8 | Repeat "A" moving in reverse line of direction. End facing partner. |

| 1-4 | Repeat "A" in line of direction. |

| 5-8 | Repeat "A" in reverse line of direction. |

NOTE: BEFORE LEARNING PART "B" STUDY VARIATION #2 WHICH IS A VERY POPULAR FORM OF PART "B."

Hold leading hand — man's L and woman's R*

B
Woman
Turns

1-2

MAN'S PART

1	2	3	1	2
SIDE	——	CLOSE;	SIDE	—— CLOSE;
←			←	
L		R	L	R

WOMAN'S PART

(one complete solo turn to her R)

1	2	3	1	2	3
SIDE	——	CLOSE;	TURN	——	TURN;
→			↘		↘
R		L	R		L

3-4

MAN'S PART

1	2	3	1	2	3
SIDE	——	CLOSE;	SIDE	TOUCH	——;
←			←	beside L	
L		R	L	(R) (no wt)	

WOMAN'S PART

(one complete turn to her R)

1	2	3	1	2	3
SIDE	——	CLOSE;	TURN	TURN	TURN;
→			↘	↘	↙
R		L	R	L	R

| 5-8 | Repeat "B" in <u>reverse</u> line of direction. <u>Change hand</u>. She turns L. |

| 1-4 | Repeat "B" in LOD. Change hand. |

| 5-8 | Repeat "B" in RLOD. Change hand. |

*Some dancers prefer to hold the trailing hand.

Go on to next page

Measures	
	(Promenade position — keep both hands joined all during "C.") (Both face LOD. R arm on top. Outside foot starts. Move in LOD 4 measures.)

	1	2	3		1	2	3
1-2	FRONT	STEP	STEP;		FRONT	TURN	HALF;
	↑	↑	↑		↑	↗	
	L	R	L		R	L	R

4 Waltzes in LOD

C

(Both face RLOD. She is now on his left side. Move backward into LOD.)

	1	2	3		1	2	3
3-4	BACK	STEP	STEP;		BACK	POINT	——;
	↓	↓	↓		↓	↑	
	L	R	L		R	(L)	

(**Face** RLOD. Inside foot starts. Move in RLOD.)

	1	2	3		1	2	3
5-6	FRONT	STEP	STEP;		FRONT	STEP	STEP;
	↑	↑	↑		↑	↑	↑
	L	R	L		R	L	R

4 in RLOD

(Face LOD. She is now on his R.)

	1	2	3		1	2	3
7-8	STEP	TURN	HALF;		BACK	POINT	——;
	↑	↶			↓	↑	
	L	R	L		R	(L)	

1-8	Repeat all of "C." Both hands are still joined.

(Closed position.)
(Man faces nearest wall.) (She starts with R foot)

	1	2	3		1	2	3
1-2	SIDE	——	CLOSE;		SIDE	TOUCH	——;
	←				←	beside L	
	L		R		L	(R)	

	1	2	3		1	2	3
3-4	SIDE	——	CLOSE;		SIDE	TOUCH	——;
	→				→	beside R	
	R		L		R	L	

D

Closed

Position

(Turn CW. Progress CCW.)
(½ turn CW . . .)   (½ turn CW . . .)

	1	2	3		1	2	3
5-6	BACK	TURN	TURN;		FRONT	TURN	TURN;
	↵	↗	↗		↗	↗	↗
	L	R	L		R	L	R

(½ turn CW . . .)   (½ turn CW . . .)

	1	2	3		1	2	3
7-8	BACK	TURN	TURN;		FRONT	TURN	TURN;
	↵	↗	↗	+	↗	↗	↗
	L	R	L		R	L	R

(These are 4 turning waltzes. To start the turn, the back of his left heel and the front of her right toe move in the line of direction. Dovetail the feet.)

1-8	Repeat "D" exactly.

VARIATIONS FOR "B"

1

Face partner.

Drop hands. Let arms float shoulder high.

Both do woman's part.

He starts on L foot and moves to L side.

Measures

2

B

(Progress in LOD. She turns R.)
(One complete solo turn away from partner.)

1	2	3		1	2	3
FRONT	HALF	TURN;		BACK	HALF	TURN;
↑	↰			↓	↳	
L	R	L		R	L	R

1-2

(Join two hands.)

1	2	3		1	2	3
SIDE	——	CLOSE;		SIDE	TOUCH	——;
←				←	(beside L)	
L		R		L	(R)	
					(no wt)	

3-4

5-8   Repeat measure 1-4 starting with other foot. Progress RLOD.

1-4   Repeat measures 1-4 in LOD.

5-8   Repeat measures 1-4 in RLOD.

References in Bibliography: 11 (p. 178), 15 (p.98), 22 (p. 185).

ALUNELUL

Romanian circle dance

Means "Little hazelnuts." Pronounced Al-loo-náy-loo.

Introduced in this country by the Romanian dance authority, Larisa Lucaci, it is a favorite because of its simplicity. Keep the steps small and light.

Records: Folk Dancer MH 1120

Folkraft 1549

Formation: Small circles of 8 to 10 dancers. Hands on neighbors' shoulders. All Start R foot.

For each dance:

1. **Say the capitalized words.**
2. **Do what you say**
3. **In the direction of the arrow**
4. **With the indicated foot.**

16

Music 2/4

Measures

1-4   Introduction — wait 8 counts.

	1	&	2	&	1	&	2	&
1-2	SIDE,	BEHIND,	SIDE,	BEHIND;	SIDE,	STAMP,	STAMP	———;
	→ R	↘ L	→ R	↘ L	→ R	(L)	(L)	(no weight on L)

	1	&	2	&	1	&	2	&
3-4	SIDE,	BEHIND,	SIDE,	BEHIND;	SIDE,	STAMP,	STAMP	———;
	← L	↙ R	← L	↙ R	← L	(R)	(R)	

5s

	1	&	2	&	1	&	2	&
5-6	SIDE,	BEHIND,	SIDE,	BEHIND;	SIDE,	STAMP,	STAMP	———;
	→ R	↘ L	→ R	↘ L	→ R	(L)	(L)	

	1	&	2	&	1	&	2	&
7-8	SIDE,	BEHIND,	SIDE,	BEHIND;	SIDE,	STAMP,	STAMP	———;
	← L	↙ R	← L	↙ R	← L	(R)	(R)	

	1	&	2	&
9	SIDE,	BEHIND,	SIDE,	STAMP;
	→ R	↘ L	→ R	(L)

	1	&	2	&
10	SIDE,	BEHIND,	SIDE,	STAMP;
	← L	↙ R	← L	(R)

3s

	1	&	2	&
11	SIDE,	BEHIND,	SIDE,	STAMP;
	→ R	↘ L	→ R	(L)

	1	&	2	&
12	SIDE,	BEHIND,	SIDE,	STAMP;
	← L	↙ R	← L	(R)

	1	&	2	&	1	&	2	&
13-14	SIDE,	STAMP,	SIDE,	STAMP;	SIDE,	STAMP,	STAMP,	———;
	→ R	(L)	← L	(R)	→ R	(L)	(L)	

1s

	1	&	2	&	1	&	2	&
15-16	SIDE,	STAMP,	SIDE,	STAMP;	SIDE,	STAMP,	STAMP,	———;
	← L	(R)	→ R	(L)	← L	(R)	(R)	

References in Bibliography: 2 (p. 42), 15 (p. 87), 18 (p. 112), 20 (p. 63).

AREDZE

South African dance

Pronounced Ah-réd-zay

This dance is one of the few set-pattern African dances which is a recreational activity. Almost all of the African dances are very personal and usually show the dancer's feelings to the village. This dance is different; it is performed for fun and is called a game dance. This dance was taught in 1969 by Odinga Lumumba, Muncie, Indiana, dancer and teacher of African dance, and is included here with his permission.

Suggested Records: Miriam Makeba, Reprise Records 0732
"Pata Pata," "Malayisha" (Reverse side)

Olatunji, Drums of Passion, Columbia CS8210
Side 1, band 4, "Gen-Go-Lo-Ba"
Side 2, band 1, "Kiyakiya"

Emancipation of Hugh Masekela, Chesa Records CHS4010
Side 1, band 3. Also side 2, band 2 (Very long.
Use only part.)

Duo Ouro Negro, the Music of Africa Today, U.A.
International UNS 15556
Side 1, band 1, "Kyrie" (13½ measures of introduction)

18

Formation: Two lines of dancers.

Men in one line facing women in other line.

Lines are about 5 feet apart.

Free foot-R.

Music 4/4, lively

Measures

The introduction will be different on different recordings. Try them and make adjustments. Keep time by bending knees.

1-2   **A**
The
Square

1	2	3	4	1	2	3	4
HOP-STEP	CLOSE	HOP-STEP	CLOSE;	SLAP	SLAP	SLAP	PIVOT;
L - R	L	L - R	L	hips	hips	hips	¼ turn L

3-8   REPEAT "A" 3 <u>more</u> times. Each dancer has moved in a large square.

1-2   **B**
Shoulders

1	2	3	4	1	2	3	4
TOUCH	STEP	TOUCH	STEP;	TOUCH	STEP	TOUCH	STEP;
(R)	R	(L)	L	(R)	R	(L)	L

While doing the "touch-step" keep the torso upright but twist or roll the shoulders* on the beat. The "touch" is done by placing the foot flat on the floor without any weight.

3-4   Dance "B" once more — each dancer passing through the other line.

A
1-8   **The**
Square

Dance "A" four times, forming the large square.

1-2   **C**
Pelvic
Tilt

(Lines moving forward toward each other)

1	2	3	4	1	2	3	4
TOUCH	STEP	TOUCH	STEP;	TOUCH	STEP	TOUCH	STEP;
(R)	R	(L)	L	(R)	R	(L)	L

On each beat the pelvis tilts forward and back. At the same time the hands are down at the sides of the body and on each beat the palms lift up as though scooping water.

3-4   Dance "C" again passing through the other line.

1-8   **A**   Dance "A" four times, forming the large square.

1-4   **B**
shoulders

Dance "B" twice
Four touch-steps moving toward other line.
Four touch-steps passing through other line.

*NOTE: The shoulder movement in "B" is an individual matter. You may pull both shoulders forward on count one and back on count two or you may alternate them or you may circle them forward or backward.

Go on to next page

Aredze   19

		1	&	2		3	&	4

1 **D Skips (Polka)**

	1	&	2		3	&	4
HOP-STEP -	CLOSE -	STEP;		HOP-STEP -	CLOSE -	STEP;	
L ↑R	L	↑R		R ↑L	R	↑L	

(This is just like our polka, but the Africans do not call it that. Arms swing freely forward and backward.)

2-4   Dance "D" 3 <u>more</u> times (8 polkas in all).

While dancing "D" move forward on the polkas counterclockwise to describe a large circle. Each dancer makes his own circle — same path as the square but round off the corners.

1-3   **C Pelvic Tilt**   Both lines move forward on first 6 touch-steps. All dancers are now in one line alternating M and W.

4   Touch-step and make a ¼ turn to R to face neighbor on R.

Touch-step making a ¼ turn to own L to face neighbor on L.

1-4   **D**   REPEAT POLKAS (8 polkas).
Describe large circle counterclockwise.

1-4   **C**   REPEAT "C" (8 touch-steps — 6 forward, 1 to R, 1 to L)

Repeat dance from beginning.
Dance to end of record.

SEQUENCE

A Square
B Shoulder (8 touch-steps)
A Square
C Pelvic tilt with hand lift (8 touch-steps)
A Square
B Shoulder — 8
D Polka — 8 in circle
C Pelvic-tilt — 8 (6 - R - L)
D Polka — 8 in circle
C Pelvic tilt — 8 (6 - R - L)

Path of dancers for "A" — Square.

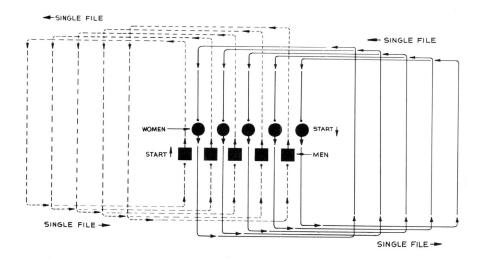

Path of dancers for "D" — Polka.

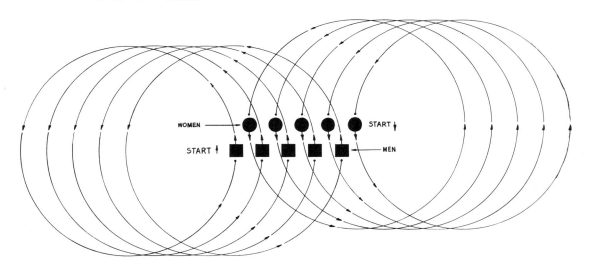

■ = men
● = women

AT VA ANI

Israeli line or circle dance

Pronounced: Aht-vah-ah-née

Choreographed by Danny Uziel. This is a lovely lyrical dance. The writer learned this at the Maine Folk Dance Camp in 1967.

Record: Israeli Folk Dance Festival (Tikva T-80)

Formation: Circle, hands joined.
Free foot — L.

Music 4/4

Measures

1-4   Introduction

<table>
<tr><td rowspan="8" style="text-align:center">

A

Brush</td><td>1-2</td><td>1</td><td>2</td><td>3</td><td>4</td><td>1</td><td>2</td><td>3</td><td>4</td></tr>
<tr><td></td><td>STEP
←
L</td><td>——</td><td>BRUSH
↗
(R) (no wt)</td><td>——;</td><td>BEND
KNEE
L</td><td>——</td><td>BEND
KNEE
L</td><td>——;</td></tr>
</table>

	1	2	3	4	1	2	3	4
3-4	STEP → R	——	BRUSH ↗ (L) (no wt)	——;	BEND KNEE R	——	BEND KNEE R	——;

(Yemenite)

	1	2	3	4	1	2	3	4
5-6	SIDE ← L	CLOSE R	CROSS ↗ L	SIDE; → R	CROSS ↗ L	SIDE; → R	CROSS ↗ L	——;

(Yemenite)

	1	2	3	4	1	2	3	4
7-8	BACK ↓ R	CLOSE beside R L	FRONT ↑ R	——;	BACK ↓ L	CLOSE beside L R	FRONT ↑ L	——;

1-8   REPEAT "A" STARTING WITH <u>RIGHT</u> FOOT.

		(upper torso erect)		(arms out)	(cross arms)		

(cross arms at chest)

		1	2	3	4	1	2	3	4
	1-2	SIDE ← L	——	CROSS ↖ R	——;	SIDE ← L	——	CROSS ↖ R	——;

B
Side

(arms out)   (full turn)   (Yemenite)   (cross arms)

		1	2	3	4	1	2	3	4
	3-4	SIDE ← L	——	TURN ↩ R	——;	SIDE ← L	CLOSE beside L R	CROSS ↗ L	——;

5-8   REPEAT "B" STARTING WITH <u>RIGHT</u> FOOT AND MOVING TO RIGHT.

NOTE: In "B," measures 1 and 2, when the arms cross on count 3
         there is a sharp abdominal contraction but the upper body
         stays erect.

BEKEDORFER

German quadrille

Pronounced Béck-eh-door-fur

This is a very enjoyable dance for eight. The steps (schottische and step-hop) are simple yet the pattern is interesting. The author learned this at the Kentucky Dance Institute Reunion in 1968.

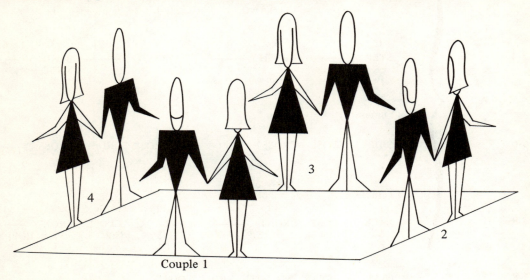

Couple 1

Record: German Folk Dances, Folkraft LP5

Formation: Four couples form a square.
　　　　　　　Woman on R of man.
　　　　　　　Use either foot.

NOTE: Learn chorus first.

　　　　Figures A, B, C are all step-hops.

Music 2/4

CHORUS

X CHORUS

CYMBAL CLAP (8 meas.)

(Couples 1 and 3 — inside hands joined)

1	2	1	2	1	2	1	2
WALK,	WALK;	WALK	———;	CLAP OWN	———;	CLAP OWN	———;

(Slash like cymbals)

1	2	1	2	1	2	1	2
STEP	HOP;	STEP	HOP;	STEP	HOP;	STEP	HOP;

(8 meas.) NOW COUPLES 2 AND 4 DO IT.

SCHOTTISCHE DOS A DOS BY COUPLES (8 meas.)

(Couples 1 and 3 — hold partner's hand)

(Pass back to back with other couple)

1	2	1	2	1	2	1	2
STEP,	STEP;	STEP,	HOP;	STEP,	STEP;	STEP,	HOP;

(Couple 1 facing couple 3)

1	2	1	2	1	2	1	2
STEP,	STEP;	STEP,	HOP;	STEP,	STEP;	STEP,	HOP;

(end in own position)

(8 meas.) NOW COUPLES 2 AND 4 DO IT.

GRAND R AND L (16 meas.)

GRAND RIGHT AND LEFT (16 step-hops; bow to partner when you meet).

(Start with R hand to partner. Continue until back home in own position.)

Music 2/4

Measures

1-4   Introduction

1-8   **A CIRCLE L then R**

(All join hands)
CIRCLE LEFT (8 step-hops)

1-8   CIRCLE RIGHT (8 step-hops)

Go on to next page

1-48	X	{ CHORUS—CYMBAL CLAP (Couples 1 and 3, then 2 and 4) SCHOTTISCHE DOS A DOS (by couples 1 and 3, then 2 and 4) GRAND RIGHT AND LEFT (step-hops)

1-8	**B**	{ PARTNERS STAR RIGHT FORWARD (8 step-hops, touch R hand and elbow)
1-8	**Star**	{ PARTNERS STAR RIGHT BACKWARD (8 step-hops)

1-48	X	{ CHORUS—CYMBAL CLAP SCHOTTISCHE DOS A DOS GRAND RIGHT AND LEFT

1-8	**C**	{ (Hold partner's two hands shoulder height) R HIPS TOUCHING (8 step-hops clockwise)
1-8	**Hip to Hip**	L HIPS TOUCHING (8 step-hops counterclockwise)

1-48	X	{ CHORUS—CYMBAL CLAP SCHOTTISCHE DOS A DOS GRAND RIGHT AND LEFT

1-8	**A**	{ (All join hands) CIRCLE LEFT (8 step-hops)
1-8	**Circle** **L then R**	CIRCLE RIGHT (8 step-hops)

```
SEQUENCE

A  Circle
X  (3 parts)
B  Star
X  (3 parts)
C  Hips
X  (3 parts)
A  Circle
```

Reference in Bibliography: 23 (Jan. 1967, p.17).

BELA RADA

Serbian line dance

Pronounced Béll-ah Ráh-dah

    This dance was introduced in this country in 1954 by Richard Crum, Pittsburgh, Pennsylvania, the noted authority on Balkan dancing, and is included here with his permission. He says the name means "Fair Rada" and comes from the first line of the song which accompanies the dance. Rada, on her way back from hoeing, meets her sweetheart who asks for a kiss.

Records: Folk Dancer MH 3023
Folkraft 1532

Formation: Open circle or line.
Joined hands are low.
The leader is at the R end.
Free foot—R.

Music 4/4

Measures

1-4   Introduction—wait 16 counts.

(Face center)   (These are reeling steps)

1	2	3	4		1	2	3	4
SIDE	BEHIND	SIDE	BEHIND;		STEP	HOP	STEP	HOP;
→	↘	→	↘		↓	↑	↓	↑
R	L	R	L		R	R	L	L

1-2

                (Scissors)   (Reeling . . . .)

1	2	3	4		1	2	3	4
STEP	HOP	KICK	KICK;		STEP	HOP	STEP	HOP;
↓	↑	↑	↑		↓	↓	↓	↑
R	R	R	L		L	L	R	R
		(step on L)	(step on R)					

3-4

         (Scissors)

KICK	KICK	LUMP	——;
↑	↑		
R	L	Both	
(step on L)	(step on R)		

5

> **SEQUENCE**
>
> 4 to right
> 3 step-hops
> Scissors
> 2 step-hops
> Scissors
> Jump

Beware — This dance takes five measures and does not fit the music.

The kicks are very small and close to the floor.

The jump is a tiny one.

For each dance:

1. Say the capitalized words.
2. Do what you say
3. In the direction of the arrow
4. With the indicated foot.

BLACK FOREST MAZURKA

German couple dance

This dance was introduced in the United States by various German groups. Mazurkas are very popular ballroom dances in Germany. Each area has its own mazurkas with special music. This one is very fast-moving.

Record: Folk Dancer MH 45-1048

Formation: Couples. Woman on R.

Face counterclockwise. Start on outside foot (M's L, W's R).

Directions given for man. <u>Woman</u> uses <u>opposite</u> foot.

Hold inside hand.

Music 3/4

Measures

1-4		Introduction	

Measures			
1-2	**A**	(Bring joined hands up) RUN TWO THREE; L R L	(Bring arms down) FOUR FIVE SIX; R L R
3-4	**Run and Turn**	(Drop hands) (Full turn; she turns R) TURN TWO THREE; L R L	(Face partner) CLAP CLAP CLAP; own hands (Wt. on both feet)
5-6	**B**	(2 mazurkas facing CCW) STEP CLOSE HOP; L R R	STEP CLOSE HOP L R R (Open dance position.)
7-8	**Mazurka and Wheel**	STEP TWO THREE; L R L	FOUR FIVE SIX; R L R (Keep open position side by side; both turn to left a complete turn.)

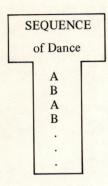

SEQUENCE
of Dance

A
B
A
B
.
.
.

Because the dance moves so fast, some groups prefer the sequence AABB.

To keep from getting dizzy, eliminate the turn in measure 3 and instead do a repeat of measure 1.

For each dance:

1. Say the capitalized words.
2. Do what you say
3. In the direction of the arrow
4. With the indicated foot.

References in Bibliography: 15 (p. 105), 18 (p. 215).

DAMBALLA

Afro-Haitian

Pronounced: Dahm-báhl-ah (name of the Voodoo Snake God)

Annette Macdonald, California State University, San Jose, has done extensive research in the field of African dancing and has arranged typical dance steps of Haiti into a set pattern for recreational dancing. She has given her permission for inclusion of Damballa, a vigorous dance that uses more body movement than the usual folk dance.

Records: Best is "Pata Pata", Miriam Makeba, Reprise Records 0732

Others — "Aki wo wo," Olatunji, Drums of Passion, Columbia CS 8210

"Malayisha," Reprise 0732

Formation: Individuals — all facing forward.

Style: Loose with bent knees. Much body movement. Pelvic and shoulder areas are most important. This dance simulates possession of the dancer by the Voodoo god.

31

Music 4/4

Measures

1-4 Introduction — wait 16 counts.

(Face R. Feet Apart. Arms overhead. Use undulating movement. Snaky. Torso waves.)

1	2	3	4	1	2	3	4
CHEST	LEADS	TORSO	DOWN;	BACK	PULLS	BODY	UP;

1-2

(Head down. Round back)

3-4 REPEAT TORSO WAVE FACING LEFT. 4 cts. down. 4 cts. up.

A
Snake Movements

(Facing R. 2 cts. down. 2 cts. up)   (Facing L. 2 down. 2 up)

1	2	3	4	1	2	3	4
TORSO	DOWN	BODY	UP;	TORSO	DOWN	BODY	UP;

5-6

(Facing R. 1 ct. down. 1 ct. up, twice) (Facing L. . . . .)

1	2	3	4	1	2	3	4
DOWN	UP	DOWN	UP;	DOWN	UP	DOWN	UP;

7-8

B
Hopping Turns

(In place; arms out to sides. . . . .)   (One complete Turn L) (Face Front)

ah	1	ah	2	ah	3	ah	4	1	2	3	4
HOP-STAMP		HOP-STAMP		HOP-STAMP		HOP-STAMP;		HOP	HOP	HOP	LUMP;
L (R)		L (R)		L (R)		L (R)		L	L	L	BOTH

1-2

(Extend R forward)
(Arms up)

3-4 Repeat HOPPING TURNS. Use other foot. Turn R.

5-6	**C Ibo Step**	(Face front. Arms and legs move together. Big movements.) (Make ½ circle with the leg)

(Face front. Arms and legs move together. Big movements.)
(Make ½ circle with the leg)

1	2	3	4	1	2	3	4
LIFT	TOUCH	LIFT	STEP;	LIFT	TOUCH	LIFT	STEP;
(R)	(R)	(R)	(Beside L) R	(L)	(L)	(L)	(Beside R) L
	(way out)				(way out)		

(Arms out)	(in)	(out)	(in)	(out)	(in)	(out)	(in)
1	2	3	4	1	2	3	4
TOUCH	STEP	TOUCH	STEP;	TOUCH	STEP	TOUCH	STEP;
(R)	(Beside L) R	(L)	(Beside R) L	(R)	R	(L)	L

(7-8 corresponds to the second table above)

1-4 B   Repeat "HOPPING TURNS."

5-8 C   Repeat "IBO STEP."   Lift legs high. Big arm movement.
Big pelvic and shoulder movements.

1 D Kicks

(Move forward.)   (¼ turn R)

1	2	3	4	&
KICK	KICK	KICK	KICK	KICK;
(L)	(R)	(L)	(R)	(L)
STEP	STEP	STEP	STEP L-R	
on R	L	R		

Arms out to sides. Bend at elbows to make figure eights. Arms sow the seeds. Feet plant them in earth.

2-4   Do "KICKS" three more times making a quarter turn R on each double kick (count "4 & .") Floor pattern is a square. This is the outline of the garden.

E Head Roll

(Face front of room)

1	2	3	4	1	2	3	4
JUMP	——	ROLL	——;	SHLDR	SHLDR	SHLDR	SHLDR;
← → Both		(Head circle)					

(Shoulder movements may be Lift-Drop or circling or shimmy.)

(5-6 corresponds to the table above)

7-8   Repeat "HEAD ROLL."
Repeat dance from beginning SNAKE movements.

```
SEQUENCE

A  Snake
B  Hopping turns
C  Ibo step
B  Hopping turns
C  Ibo step
D  Kicks
E  Head roll
```

DEBKA DAYAGIM
Israeli line dance

Pronounced Deb-ka Die-ah-ghéem

Choreographed by Shalom Hermon. Music by Aldema.

    Mr. Hermon describes Debka Dayagim as follows: "It was choreographed as part of a folk-dance suite of concert dances. This dance, the second in the suite, was a men's dance. The first was a dance for women and the third was a couple dance . . . . Dayagim in Hebrew means fisherman." The dancers themselves made the dance a "folkdance" by moving it from the concert stage to the "folk."

    The dance is arranged from a description by Fred Berk (in direction pamphlet which comes with record). It is reproduced here by permission of Shalom Hermon.

Record: Debka (Tikva T-100)

Formation: Line.

              Hands joined.

              Line of direction counterclockwise (CCW).

              Free foot — R.

Music 2/4

Measures

1-8   Introduction

(Lean fwd)   (Up tall . . . .)

	1	2	1	2	1	2	1	2
1-4 **A** **2 Runs**	RUN, ↗ R	RUN; ↗ L	STEP, ↗ R	HOP; R	STEP, ↗ L	HOP; L	STEP, ↗ R	HOP; R
5-8 **3 Step-hops**	RUN, ↗ L	RUN; ↗ R	STEP, ↗ L	HOP; L	STEP, ↗ R	HOP; R	STEP, ↗ L	HOP; L

(Face center. Lean forward on back kick. On each kick, hop on supporting foot.)

	1	2	1	2	1	2	1	2
1-4 **B** **Kicks**	STEP, → R	KICK; ↑ (L)	STEP, ↗ L	KICK; ↓ (R)	STEP, → R	KICK; ↑ (L)	STEP, ↗ L	KICK; ↓ (R)
		Hop R (arms up)		Hop L (arms down)				

5-8   Repeat the four kicks. Line continues moving counterclockwise.

1-8   **A**   **Runs**   Repeat "A" exactly as above.

Music 6/4

(Face center)

	1	2	3	4	5	6
1 measure **Double Tcherkessia**	FRONT, ↖ R	BACK, ↘ L	STEP, beside L R	FRONT, ↗ L	BACK, ↙ R	STEP; beside R L

C

Music 2/4

(Face center)

	1	2	1	2	1	2	1	2
1-4 **Double Hops**	CROSS, ↖ R	HOP; R	CROSS, ↗ L	HOP; L	BACK, ↓ R	HOP; R	BACK, ↓ L	HOP; L
5-8	STEP, ↑ R	HOP; R	TOUCH, ↓ (L)	HOP; R	TOUCH, ↓ (L)	HOP; R	STEP, ↑ L	HOP; L
			(no wt)		(no wt)			

(While "touching," hop on supporting foot.)

DOUDLEBSKA POLKA
Czechoslovakian mixer

Pronounced Dood-léb-skah Polka.

Introduced in this country by Jeannette Novak, the dance is an enjoyable mixer and is a favorite recreational dance for changing partners.

Records: Folk Dancer MH 3016

Folkraft 1413

Educational Dance Recordings FD-2

Formation: Couples, closed position.

Line of direction counterclockwise (CCW).

Free foot — Man's L, woman's R.

Music 2/4

Measures

1-4   Introduction (wait)

1-16   A   { POLKA TURNS (clockwise turn moving CCW)   } one <u>long</u> phrase
                                (social dance position)

1-16   B   SING, "LAH, LAH, LAH" (open social dance position)

Walk forward around circle. Man stretches L hand forward to touch L shoulder of man ahead.

At end of "B," lady turns sharply right to face reverse line of direction.

one <u>long</u> phrase

1-16   C   MEN CLAP RHYTHM — quick, quick, slow. (Men in single circle.)

1	&	2
clap (own hands)	clap (own hands)	out (neighbors' hands)

LADIES POLKA FORWARD (clockwise, on outside of men's circle)

one <u>long</u> phrase

At end of "C," men make sharp turn to face ladies and begin dance again with new lady who happens to be there.

References in Bibliography: 2 (p. 53), 11 (p. 195), 15 (p. 138), 18 (p. 170), 20 (p. 33).

EREV BA

Israeli circle dance

Pronounced Aír-ev Bah (means Evening Comes)

Choreographed by Yoav Ashriel, Givatayim, Israel.

Music by Aryeh Levanon.

    The dance, choreographed in 1960, was based on the song that won the first prize in the Annual Music Festival in honor of Israel's Independence Day. It is reproduced here by permission of Yoav Ashriel. Mr. Ashriel describes the dance as follows: "I was especially impressed by the beauty of the melody and the gentle, slow tempo. I tried to make it possible for the dancers to express their own quiet and tranquility in this dance — a quiet and tranquility that each feels in his heart of a calm, pastoral evening in Israel. In this dance one can feel the Mediterranean atmosphere in the steps."

Record: Israel Sings, Vanguard VRS-9118

Formation: Circle. Joined hands low.

               Free foot — R.

Music 4/4

Measures

1-4   Introduction (wait)

1-2   **A**

1	2	3	4	1	2	3	4
SIDE	CROSS	BACK	SIDE;	CROSS	AND	CROSS	———;
→	↗	↙	←	↖	(close)	↖	
R	L	R	L	R	L	R	

Crossover and Grapevine

(This is a grapevine)

3-4

1	2	3	4	1	2	3	4
BACK	SIDE	FRONT	SIDE:	BACK	SIDE	FRONT	———;
↘	→	↗	→	↘	→	↗	
L	R	L	R	L	R	L	

1-4   REPEAT "A" EXACTLY.

B
Turns

(Drop hands — solo turn) (Double tcherkessia . . . .)
(3-step-turn)

1-2

1	2	3	4	1	IN	3	4
SIDE	TURN	TURN	CROSS:	BACK	PLACE	CROSS	BACK;
→	↷	↷	↗	↙	(beside R)	↖	↘
R	L	R	L	R	L	R	L

3-4   REPEAT "B" EXACTLY.

C
Moving Sideward Toward Center

(R shoulder toward center)

1-2

1	2	3	4	1	2	3	4
SIDE	CROSS	SIDE	CROSS;	SIDE	CROSS	SIDE	CLOSE;
→	↗	→	↗	→	↗	→	(beside R)
R	L	R	L	R	L	R	L

(Move away from center. . . . .) (a complete turn into LOD)

3-4

1	2	3	4	1	2	3	4
CROSS	SIDE	CROSS	SIDE;	CROSS	SIDE	TURN	TURN;
↖	←	↖	←	↖	←	↷	↷
R	L	R	L	R	L	R	L

                  REPEAT DANCE FROM BEGINNING.

Final Ending — The record Vanguard VRS-9118 allows time to do the dance three times with a little music left over for a final ending.

(a complete turn)

1-2

1	2	3	4	1	2	3	4
SIDE	CROSS	BACK	SIDE;	CROSS	BACK	TURN	TURN;
→	↗	↙	←	↖	↘	↷	↷
R	L	R	L	R	L	R	L

3-4   REPEAT "ENDING" EXACTLY.

Reference in Bibliography: 22 (p. 148).

FAMILIE SEKSTUR

Danish mixer

Pronounced: Fah-mill-yeh Sex-toor

   Jane Farwell, the noted recreation specialist, and Gordon Tracie, the authority on Scandinavian dancing, introduced this dance in the United States. Like many other Danish dances this one includes a game element. It is a gay playful dance which is still seen at many Scandinavian social gatherings. The middle of the circle is the Lost and Found department. The dance is included here with permission of Jane Farwell, Dodgeville, Wisconsin.

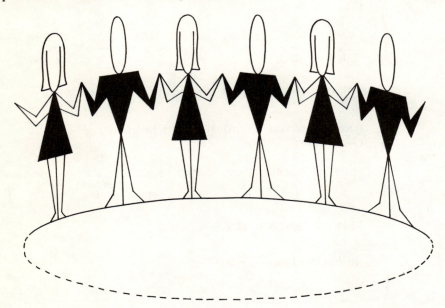

Record: Aqua Viking V400

   Lindon 703

   RCA LPM 9910

Formation: Single circle of couples.

   All face center.

   Woman on R of man.

   Hands joined shoulder high.

   Free foot — R.

Music 2/4

Measures

1-2   **A**

Introduction done only <u>once</u> – at beginning of dance. Buzz Steps (16 in all)

(Circle moves to left)

1		ah	2		ah
CROSS	——	SIDE	CROSS	——	SIDE;
↖		←	↖		←
R		L	R		L
1		ah	2		ah
CROSS	——	SIDE	CROSS	——	SIDE;
↖		←	↖		←
R		L	R		L

3-8   Repeat "A" 3 more times.

1-2   **B**

Into Center and Out

(Gradually raising joined hands)   (Nod head)

1	2	1	2
WALK	TWO;	THREE	FOUR;
↑	↑	↑	↑
R	L	R	L

(Lower joined hands to shoulder height)   (Nod to partner)

3-4

1	2	3	4
BACK	TWO;	THREE	FOUR;
↓	↓	↓	↓
R	L	R	L

5-8   Repeat "B" one more time.

1-8   **C**

Grand R & L

Grand right and left seven.
Face partner and join R hands. This is number "one."
Keep moving in direction you are facing (men counterclockwise, women clockwise).
Alternate hands and count each person you meet until you come to number "seven." Keep number "seven."

1-8   **D**

Buzz Swing

Hold new partner in modified social dance position – R hip to R hip.
Joined hands held straight out to side.
Buzz step same as in "A." At end of phrase put woman on right and join all hands for walking in and out.

REPEAT ENTIRE DANCE FROM "B."

References in Bibliography: 9 (p. 20), 11 (p. 206), 18 (p. 79).

GERAKINA

Greek line dance

Pronounced Gair-ah-kée-nah

The origins of this dance are vague; they probably stem from some religious ritual. Gerakina is a girl's name which is common in Macedonia, the region of this dance.

This dance uses 7/8 music. The counts are divided into a rhythm of

1-2-3	4-5	6-7
SLOW	QUICK	QUICK

It may be less complicated for the inexperienced dancer if he thinks of this as a 1-2-3 rhythm with count "1" being a little longer than the others.

Records: Folkraft 1060

Columbia 10073

Formation: Line. Hands joined.

Elbows bent.

Move counterclockwise (CCW).

Free foot — R.

42

Music 7/8   Rhythm is <u>slow</u>-quick-quick.

Measures

Music has no introduction.

		(Face R)			(Face center . . . .)		
		(slow)	(q)	(q)	(s)	(q)	(q)
1-2	**A**	1-2	3	4-5	6-7	1-2-3	4-5	6-7
		STEP	HOP	STEP	SIDE;	BEHIND	BRUSH	TOUCH;
		↗		↗	→	↘	←··	←··
		R	R	L	R	L	(R)	(R)
			(very quick)				(no wt)	

3-8   Dance "A" three more times (continue moving CCW).

		(Face R, hands low)					
		(slow)	(quick)	(quick)	(slow)	(quick)	(quick)
						(heel out)	(heel in)
9-10	**B**	STEP	STEP	STEP;	STEP	WIGGLE	WIGGLE;
		↗	↗	↗	↗	··→	←··
		R	L	R	L	(R) (no wt)	(R) (no wt)

11-12   Repeat "B" continue moving CCW. On last wiggle, face center.

13-14   Repeat "B" moving to center of circle. Raise hands.

		(Lower hands slowly)					
15-16		BACK	QUICK	QUICK;	BACK	QUICK	QUICK;
	Scissors	↓	↓	↓	↓	↓	↓
		R	L	R	L	R	L
		(kick L	(kick R	(kick L	(kick other foot forward)		
		fwd)	fwd)	fwd)			

		(R foot in front)					
		s	q	q	s	q	q
17-18		WIGGLE	IN	OUT	IN	OUT	BRUSH
	Long	··→	←··	··→	←··	··→	↗
	Wiggle	(R heel	(R)	(R)	(R)	(R)	(R) (no wt)
		out)					
		(no wt)					

		(Drop hands)					
		(One complete solo turn in 6 steps . . . .)					
19-20	**Turn**	TURN	QUICK	QUICK;	SLOW	QUICK	QUICK
		↷					
		R	L	R	L	R	L

On measures 19 and 20 the left arm is held straight forward with the palm away from body, fingers pointing upward. The back of the R hand is placed low on the back of the R hip.

References in Bibliography: 11 (p. 209), 13 (p. 30 "c").

GODEČKI ČAČAK

Serbian-Bulgarian

Pronounced Go-détch-kee Chah-cháhk

   This dance was introduced by Richard Crum who brought many Balkan dances to American folk dancers. The dance has many variations—all of them interesting and exciting.

Record: Du-Tam 1002

Formation: Short lines of 3 or 4.
              Belt hold - L hand over.

Pattern of dance: <u>Two</u> measures of a figure followed by
              <u>Three</u> measures of another figure.

Music 2/4

Measures

1-4   Introduction — wait

1-5   A   { (Face right)
1	2	1	2
LEAP	LEAP;	LEAP	LEAP;
↗	↗	↗	↗
R	L	R	L

(Face center)
1	2	1	2	1	2
STEP-LIFT;		STEP-LIFT;		STEP-LIFT	
→	↗	←	↖	→	↗
R	(L)	L	(R)	R	(L)
(Hop on R)		(Hop on L)		(Hop on R)	

6-20   Dance "A" three <u>more</u> times (L, R, L). Reverse feet and arrows each time.

1-5   B   Hop-Step Step   { (Face center)
1	&	2	1	&	2
KNEE-STEP-STEP;			HOP-STEP-STEP;		
↙		(In place)	(In place)		
(R)	- R -	L	L	- R -	L
(Hop on L)					

(Open Close   Open Close   Open Close)
1	2	1	2	1	2
JUMP CLICK;		JUMP CLICK;		JUMP CLICK;	
↙↘	→←	↙↘	→←	↙↘	→←
Both	Both	Both	Both	B	B

6-20   Dance "B" three <u>more</u> times. Reverse feet each time. On HOP, twist free knee in front.

1-5   C   Heel-scuff   {
(three pas-de-bas)
1	2	1	2	1	&	2	1	&	2	1	&	2
STAMP	BRUSH;	HOP	STEP;	SIDE-FRONT-BACK;			SIDE-FRONT-BACK;			SIDE-FRONT-BACK		
→	↙		↓	→	↗	↙	←	↖	↘	→	↗	↙
R	(L)	R	L	R	- L -	R	L	- R -	L	R	- L -	R

6-20   Repeat "C" three <u>more</u> times (L, R, L). Reverse feet and arrows each time.

1-5   D   Step Draw   {
(Bend from waist . . . . .)   (Up tall — three pas-de-bas)
1	2	1	2	1	&	2	1	&	2	1	&	2
STEP	DRAW;	STEP	DRAW;	SIDE-FRONT-BACK;			SIDE-FRONT-BACK;			SIDE-FRONT-BACK;		
↑	to R	↑	to R	→	↗	↙	←	↖	↘	→	↗	↙
R	L	R	L	R	- L -	R	L -	R -	L	R	- L -	R

(High prance backward)   (Three pas-de-bas)
1	2	1	2	1	&	2	1	&	2	1	&	2
LEAP	LEAP;	LEAP	LEAP;	SIDE-FRONT-BACK;			SIDE-FRONT-BACK;			SIDE-FRONT-BACK;		
↓	↓	↓	↓	←	↖	↘	→	↗	↙	←	↖	↘
L	R	L	R	L	- R -	L	R	- L -	R	L	- R -	L

6-10   (as shown above)

11-20   Repeat "D" exactly.

#1 VARIATION FOR "A"

(Face center)

1-5   A

```
        1    2      1    2    1  &  2      1  &  2      1  &  2
        LEAP LEAP;  LEAP LEAP LEAP-RUN-RUN; LEAP-RUN-RUN; LEAP-RUN-RUN;
        ↗    ↗      ↗    ↗    ↗   ↗  ↗      ↗   ↗  ↗      ↗   ↗  ↗
        R    L      R    L    R - L - R     L - R - L     R - L - R
```

6-20   Repeat "A" to L, R, L.

#2 VARIATION FOR "A"

```
1-5 A          (Face right)                    (Face center)
    Russian    1  &  2      1  &  2            1    2     1    2     1    2
    Two-Step   LEAP-RUN-RUN; LEAP-RUN-RUN;     STEP HOP;  STEP HOP;  STEP HOP;
               ↗   ↗  ↗      ↗   ↗  ↗           →          ←          →
               R - L - R     L - R - L         R    R     L    L     R    R
```

6-20   Repeat "A" to L, R, L (four times in all).

#1 VARIATION FOR "B"

```
              (Face  center)          (Three  pas-de-bas)
1-5  B        1  &  2   1  &  2   1  &  2       1  &  2      1  &  2       1  &  2
              HOP-STEP-STEP; HOP-STEP-STEP; SIDE-FRONT-BACK; SIDE-FRONT-BACK; SIDE-FRONT-BACK;
                   →            →         →    ↗   ↖    ←   ↗    ↗   ↖
              L    R    L   L   R    L   R    L    R    L    R    L    R
```

6-20   Dance "B" three more times. Reverse feet and arrows each time.

NOTE: The dance is built on a pattern of two plus three.

GRAZIELLA MAZURKA

Italian ballroom dance

Pronounced Grah-tzee-élla

Performed in many countries, mazurkas are usually couple dances of the ballroom variety. This particular mazurka has a feeling of smoothness with a floating quality. Some dancers flirt when they do this dance.

This dance was introduced into this country many years ago by Millie von Konsky of the Oakland Recreation Department, Oakland, California, and is included here with her permission.

Record: Victor RCA 25-7061

Formation: Varsovienne position.

Face CCW around room.

Both start with R foot.

Style — soft and lyrical.

Music 3/4

Measures

NO INTRODUCTION IN MUSIC.

	1	2	3		1	2	3
1-2	STEP	SWING	———;		STEP	TOUCH	———;
A-1	→	↗			←	(Beside L)	
Step	R	(L)			L	(R)	
Swings							

(Move toward wall . . . .)

	1	2	3		1	2	3
3-4	WALK	WALK	WALK;		WALK	WALK	———;
	↗	↗	↗		↗	↗	
	R	L	R		L	R	

		MAN'S PART (balance forward and back)							WOMAN'S PART

MAN'S PART (balance forward and back)

	1	2	3	1	2	3
	in	in		in	in
STEP	PLACE	PLACE;	STEP	PLACE	PLACE
↑			↓		
L	R	L	R	L	R

WOMAN'S PART
Circle the man CCW with 6 walks. Then drop L hand and turn individually with 6 steps and resume varsovienne position.

5-6 **A-2 Woman Goes Around Man**

	1	2	3	1	2	3
	in	in		in	in
STEP	PLACE	PLACE;	STEP	PLACE	PLACE;
↑			↓		
L	R	L	R	L	R

7-8

NOTE: From here to end of dance, do not drop either hand. Hold them loosely. Experienced dancers should do A-2 without dropping either hand.

(Both face LOD)
(L mazurkas to center of hall)

1-2

1	2	3	1	2	3
STEP	CLOSE	HOP;	STEP	CLOSE	HOP;
←			←		
L	R	R	L	R	R

3-4 **B Mazurka to Center**

1	2	3	1	2	3	(Keep hands joined)
STEP	CLOSE	HOP;	STEP	STEP	STEP;	(She is now on his L)
←						(In place, turning to face wall)
L	R	R	L	R	L	

(R mazurkas toward wall)

5-6

1	2	3	1	2	3
STEP	CLOSE	HOP;	STEP	CLOSE	HOP;
→			→		
R	L	L	R	L	L

(He turns her to her L)

7-8

1	2	3	1	2	3
STEP	CLOSE	HOP;	STEP	STEP	STEP;
→				(In place)	
R	L	L	R	L	R

(End facing each other)
(Man's back to center)
(Joined R hands on top)

	C Together and Apart	(Balance forward then backward)					

1-4   **C Together and Apart**

(Balance forward then backward)

1	2	3	1	2	3
TOGETHER	STEP	STEP;	APART	STEP	STEP;
↑	beside L	beside R	↓	beside R	beside L
L	R	L	R	L	R

(She makes one complete turn to her R under their joined hands)

1	2	3	1	2	3
STEP	TWO	THREE;	APART	STEP	STEP
			↓		
L	R	L	R	L	R

5-8

1	2	3	1	2	3
TOGETHER	STEP	STEP;	APART	STEP	STEP;
			↓		
L	R	L	R	L	R

(She makes one complete turn to her L under their joined hands)

1	2	3	1	2	3
STEP	TWO	THREE;	APART	STEP	TOUCH;
			↓		(Beside L)
L	R	L	R	L	(R)

1-2   **D Mazurka Around Partner**

(L shoulders adjacent)

1	2	3	1	2	3
STEP	CLOSE	HOP;	STEP	CLOSE	HOP;
↗			↗		
R	L	L	R	L	L

(Face partner)

(Continue around partner CCW) (Partners have exchanged places)

3-4

1	2	3	1	2	3
WALK	WALK	WALK;	STEP	SIDE	TOUCH;
↑	↑	↑	↑	→	←··
R	L	R	L	R	(L)

5-6

(R shoulders adjacent. Move CW around partner)

1	2	3	1	2	3
STEP	CLOSE	HOP;	STEP	CLOSE	HOP;
↖			↖		
L	R	R	L	R	R

7-8

(Raise joined R hands)
(She turns into varsovienne position)

1	2	3	1	2	3
WALK	WALK	WALK;	STEP	STEP	TOUCH;
↑	↑	↑			
L	R	L	R	L	(R)

(End in original position. Face CCW.)

Reference in Bibliography: 23 (Dec. 1961)

HAROA HAKTANA

Israeli Individual Dance

Pronounced Hah-ro-áh Hock-tah-náh. Means *"Little Shepherdess."*

This marvelously exciting dance was choreographed by Jonathan Karmon. On the west coast of the United States this dance is nicknamed "The Flying Dance."

Record: Dance Along with Sabras, Tikva T-69, side 2, band 3.

Formation: Individuals — start facing center.

Movement is counterclockwise around room.

Start with arms down and close to body as though holding a shepherd's crook.

NOTE: To Facilitate learning part "A" do a step-hop instead of a jump-hop.

Step on the foot that does the hop.

Start with R as the foot free.

Music 4/4

Measures

1-4 Introduction — wait 16 counts.

A
Half-turns

(Face center)	(Half-turn R)	(Face out)	(Half-turn L)	(Face in)	(Half-turn L)	(Face out)	(Half-turn R)
1	2	3	4	1	2	3	4
JUMP	HOP	LUMP	HOP;	LUMP	HOP	LUMP	HOP;
← →	↷	← →	↶	← →	↶	← →	↷
Both	R	Both	L	Both	R	Both	L

1-2 (above)

3-4 (below)

(Face in)	(Half-turn R)	(Face out)	(Half-turn R)	(Two pas-de-bas facing center)				
1	2	3	4	1	&	2	3	&	4
LUMP	HOP	LUMP	HOP;	SIDE-FRONT-BACK			SIDE-FRONT-BACK;	
← →	↷	← →	↷	→ ↗ ↙			← ↖ ↘	
Both	R	Both	L	R - L - R			L - R - L	

(Snap fingers) (high)   (Snap fingers) (high)

> NOTE: Sequence for the half-turns.
> One half-turn to R.
> Two half-turns to L (makes a full turn).
> Three half-turns to R (makes a turn and a half).
> All half-turns progress counterclockwise around the room.

5-8 **A** REPEAT "A" EXACTLY

B
In-out

1-3

(Move to center) (Turn L shoulder to center)				(Move back) (Turn R shoulder to center)				(Face center) (2 pas-de-bas or 2 balances)				
1	2	3	4	1	2	3	4	1	&	2	3	&	4
STEP	HOP	STEP	HOP;	STEP	HOP	STEP	HOP;	SIDE-FRONT-BACK			SIDE-FRONT-BACK;	
↑R	R	↑L	L	↓R	R	↓L	L	→ ↗ ↙			← ↖ ↘	
								R - L - R			L - R - L	

(Snap fingers) (high)   (Snap fingers) (high)

4-6 **B** REPEAT "B" EXACTLY

7-8 **B′**
Break

(Face center)				(Hands up)		(Palms down toward floor—strong)		
1	2	3	4	1	2	3	4	
STEP	SWING	KICK	KICK;	STEP	SWING	TOUCH	——— ;	
in place	↥	↧	↧	←	↥	(Beside L)		
R	(L)	(R)	(L)	L	(R)	(R)		
	(hop on R)	(step on L)	(step on R)	(hop on L)				

(Hands are low and follow the movement of the swing and kicks)

HILLS OF HABERSHAM

U.S. — Waltz contra dance

Choreographed by Mary and Fred Collette.

Dedicated to the beauty of the mountains of North Georgia, the title is from "Song of the Chattahoochee" by Sidney Lanier. Mrs. Lloyd Shaw describes this dance in the following manner.

"Habersham is a hilly county in northeast Georgia, where the great Chattahoochee River rises and starts to the Gulf. This longways dance catches the running and turning, the whispering at the bank, the ebb and flow and repeat of a great river. The two lines cross and re-cross, eddy back and return, balance in little crosswise cascades, spin in little whirlpools, and return to place."

The dance is arranged from the dance description of Mary and Fred Collette of Atlanta, Georgia, and reproduced here with their permission.

Brief reminders about contra dancing.

Head of the Hall is the wall where the music is located.

"Up" or "above" is toward the head of the hall.

"Down" or "below" is toward the foot of the line.

In contra formation two lines are facing.

Men are all in one line with L shoulders toward the Head of the Hall.

Women are in opposite line facing partner.

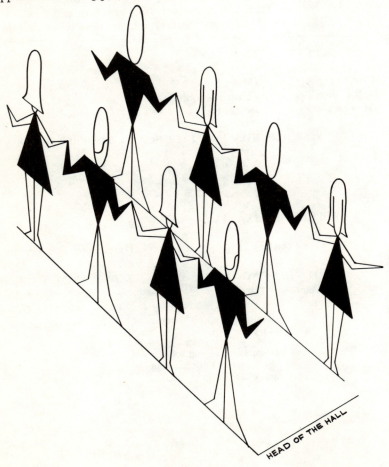

HEAD OF THE HALL

52

"Actives" work themselves <u>down</u> the set. They remain "actives" until they get to the foot and then become "neutrals."

"Inactives" work themselves <u>up</u> the set. They remain "inactives" until they get to the head and then become "neutrals."

Both at the head and at the foot there will be a neutral couple every other time the dance is repeated. They should exchange places with partner and be ready to become "active" at the head and "inactive" at the foot.

Records: Shaw X-75.

Columbia DX 1803, "Royal Cotillion 3."

Or any moderate tempo 32 measure waltz.

Formation: Contra, 6-9 couples.

Couples 1, 3, 5, 7 cross over (change places with partners). These are actives.

All face partners.

Join hands shoulder high along two lines.

Elbows bent.

All start R foot.

When dancers have no specific action, they should balance sideward in place. When "actives" go down outside and up center, the "inactives" do R — arch* then L — arch, etc. moving up sideward to head of hall with wider step in that direction sufficiently to hold set in place.

Music 3/4

Measures

1-4   Introduction — bow to partner

1-2   **Crossover**

(Drop hands)
(Pass partner by R shoulder)

WALK	TWO	THREE;	FOUR	FIVE	SIX;
↑	↑	↑	↑	↑	↑
R	L	R	L	R	L

3-4   **Balance**

(Join hands in long line — face out)

1	2	3		1	2	3
STEP	ARCH*	——;		STEP	ARCH*	——;
→				←		
R	(L)			L	(R)	
(Look R)				(Look L)		

A

5-6   **Turn**

(Drop hands. Half turn solo)

1	2	3	1	2	3
TURN	TO	YOUR;	RI -	I -	IGHT
↷					
R	L	R	L	R	L

7-8   **Balance**

(Join hands in long line — face in)

1	2	3	1	2	3
STEP,	ARCH	——;	STEP,	ARCH	——;
→			←		
R	(L)		L	(R)	
	(Look R)			(Look L)	

1-8   Repeat "A" to finish in original position.

*See page 55.

Go on to next page

1-4	Roll Out	(<u>Actives only</u>) (Separate)

(<u>Actives only</u>)   (Separate)

FACE   UP;   ROLL   OUT;   PASS   TWO;   COME   IN;
1   2   3   1   2   3   1   2   3   1   2   3
R -L - R   L - R - L   R - L - R   L - R - L

1-4   Roll Out

5-6   Come Up

(Active lady is on L of her partner)
GO   UP   TO;   PAIR   BELOW YOU;
1   2   3   1   2   3
R - L - R   L - R - L

7-8   Balance

(Four in line – join hands – face up)
1   2   3   1   2   3

STEP,   ARCH ——;   STEP,   ARCH ——;
→
R   (L)   ←
                    L   (R)
(Look R)   (Look L)

B

1-2   Wheel

(Actives as a unit)
(One complete turn with six steps)
(Men back up. Women go forward.)
1   2   3   1 2 3
THE   AC-TIVES;   WHEEL;

3-4   Balance

(Four in line – join hands – face up)
1   2   3   1   2   3

STEP,   ARCH ——;   STEP   ARCH ——;
→
R   (L)   ←
                    L   (R)
(Look R)   (Look L)

5-6   Cast Off

(Actives)
(Drop partner's hand. Go around one.)
1   2   3   1   2   3
    CAST;   OFF;

7-8   Balance

(Join hands in contra line. Face partner.)
1   2   3   1   2   3

STEP,   ARCH ——;   STEP;   ARCH ——;
→
R   (L)   ←
                    L   (R)
(Look R)   (Look L)

(Actives end up one place "below" their starting position.)

In part "B" the actives face "up" and continue turning out until they are facing "down." The actives go down outside of the set until they pass two inactives who are doing waltz balances in place. Then the actives come in, meet partner, join near hands and go up the inside of the set until they are standing between the man and woman who were below them. Then form a line of four facing "up" with hands joined shoulder high.

Step R and arch means to step on R foot and arch the L foot to the supporting R foot by having the arch of the L foot touch the heel of the R foot with L toe on floor and L heel slightly off floor, like this:

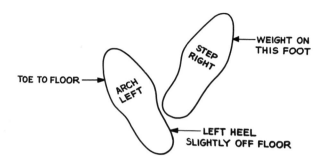

For each dance:

1. Say the capitalized words.
2. Do what you say
3. In the direction of the arrow
4. With the indicated foot.

HOPPA HEY

Israeli dance

Pronounced Hópe-ah Hay

Choreographed by Rivka Sturman, one of the outstanding choreographers of Israeli dances.

    This dance is very vigorous and enjoyable and is a favorite of men and boys. This dance was taught by Fred Berk at the Blue Star Israeli Folk Dance Camp in 1966.

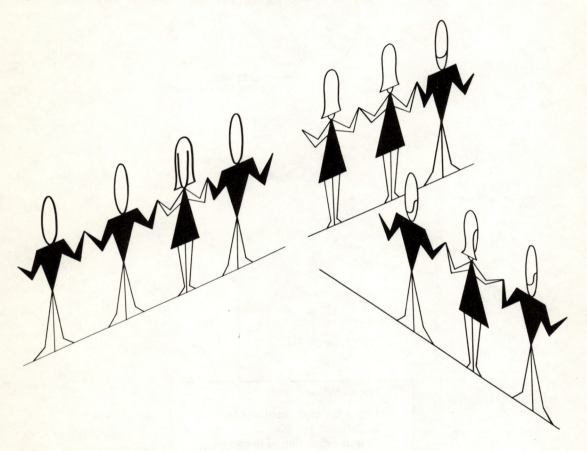

Record: Dance for Fun, Tikva T-104

Formation: Spokes of a wheel.

            3 to 5 dancers stand side by side.

            They are one spoke. Face counterclockwise (CCW).

            All start with R foot.

NOTE: Learn chorus first.

Music 4/4

Measures

1   Little drum beats.

1-4   Introduction — wait.

1-2   **A**

	1	2	3	4	1	2	3	4
	RUN	TWO	THREE	FOUR;	CROSS	HOP	CROSS	HOP;
	↑	↑	↑	↑	↖		↗	
	R	L	R	L	R	R	L	L

3-4   **Chorus**

	RUN	TWO	THREE	FOUR;	KICK	KICK	KICK	KICK;
	↑	↑	↑	↑	⋮	⋮	↓	↓
	R	L	R	L	(L)	(R)	(L)	(R) (wt is on L)
					(Step R)	(Step L)	(Step R)	(Step L)

5-8   REPEAT "A" AND "CHORUS"

9-10   **B**

(Drop hands and face center, one behind the other)

				HALF-TURN;	HALF-TURN			
	STEP	CLAP	SIDE			HOP	FRONT	BACK;
	↗		←	↰	↰		↑	↓
	R		L	R	L	L	R	L

(3-step turn to L . . . .)

11-12 **Chorus**

(Face CCW, join hands)

	RUN	TWO	THREE	FOUR;	KICK	KICK	KICK	KICK;
	↑	↑	↑	↑	⋮	↑	↓	↓
	R	L	R	L	(L)	(R)	(L)	(R) (wt is on L)

13-16   REPEAT "B" AND "CHORUS"

Repeat dance from beginning.

Final Ending — comes just as dancers are ready to start "B."

	1	2	3	4	1	
Drum beats —	STEP	CLAP	STEP	CLAP;	STAMP	(Shout "Hey" on stamp. Throw both
	↗		↖		↑	arms up and out during shout.)
	R		L		R	

HORA
Israeli circle dance

Pronounced Hór-ah

   This dance, which probably originated in Romania, is considered the national Jewish dance. The Hora and the Oro and the Kolo dances have a similarity in formation and step patterns. Most of these dances are broken circle dances which use simple step patterns that are repeated over and over.

Suggested record: Hava Nagella, Folkraft 1110. There are many others.

Formation: Circle.

No partners.

Hands on neighbor's shoulders.

Free foot — R when moving right.

Music 2/4

Measures

1-4   Introduction — wait.

1-3

	1	2	1	2	1	2
	SIDE,	BEHIND;	SIDE,	HOP;	SIDE,	HOP;
	→	↘	→		←	
	R	L	R	R	L	L

The dance consists of one schottische sideways to the right and one step-hop to the left. May start on L foot and move to the left.

When using concentric circles, one circle may move right and one circle may move left.

VARIATIONS

#1

1-3

$\left\{\vphantom{\begin{matrix}a\\b\end{matrix}}\right.$

SIDE	BEHIND;	JUMP	HOP;	JUMP	HOP;
→	↘				
R	L	Both	R	Both	L

#2

1-3

$\left\{\vphantom{\begin{matrix}a\\b\end{matrix}}\right.$

SIDE	BEHIND;	JUMP	HOP;	STEP–STEP–STEP;		
→	↘			(in place)		
R	L	Both	R	L	R	L

HASAPIKOS

Many countries have dances that are exactly like the Hora or are very similar to the Hora, in that they use six actions in three measures of 2/4 music. The music and styling are characteristic of the specific country. So now you know hundreds of dances.

The Greek Hora is called <u>HASAPIKOS</u>. It is very fast moving. The only difference between HASAPIKOS and the HORA is the second action. In HASAPIKOS, step across in front.

Variations for HASAPIKOS: (Leader — at right end — decides when to change.)
#1 — A complete solo turn <u>Right</u> on second action.
#2 — Sliding sidewards to the <u>Right</u>. This is accompanied by "hissing" sounds made by dancers.

Record: Rendezvous in Greece, Roulette R-25229, Side 1, Band 4.

Or any fast Hasapiko.

References in Bibliography: 11 (p. 218), 15 (p. 71), 16 (p. 159).

HORA NIRKODA

Let Us Dance the Hora
Israeli circle dance

Pronounced Hora Neer-kó-dah.

Choreographed by Yoav Ashriel, Givatayim, Israel.

Music by Mark Lavry.

According to Yoav Ashriel, "This dance was choreographed about twelve years ago. I wanted to express the joy and enthusiasm of the robust Israeli sabras who rejoiced in their togetherness. The wide-sweeping movements of the dance characterize this feeling as seen in the upraised movements of the arms. The rhythm of Mark Lavry's music lends a special tempo to the music which serves to further enthuse the eager dancers."

The dance was arranged from a description by Fred Berk (in direction pamphlet which comes with record) and is reproduced here by permission of Yoav Ashriel.

Record: Debka (Tikva T-100)

Formation: Circle. Hands joined.

Free foot — R.

For each dance:

1. Say the capitalized words.
2. Do what you say
3. In the direction of the arrow
4. With the indicated foot.

Music 4/4

Measures

1-2   Introduction

A
Mayim
2 Times

1-2

(This is a Mayim step . . . .)

1	2	3	4	1	2	3	4
FRONT	SIDE	BEHIND	LEAP;	FRONT	SIDE	BEHIND	LEAP;
↖	←	↙	←	↖	←	↙	←
R	L	R	L	R	L	R	L

3-4

1	2	3	4	1	2	3	4
IN	HOP	IN	HOP;	WALK	TWO	THREE	FOUR;
↑		↑		↓	↓	↓	↓
R	R	L	L	R	L	R	L

5-8   REPEAT "A" EXACTLY.

B
Leap –
Run
2 Times

1-2

(Hold hands – face R.)   (Drop hands. Turn individually)
         (One complete 4-step-turn)

1	2	3	4	1	2	3	4
LEAP	RUN	LEAP	RUN;	TURN	TURN	TURN	STEP;
↗	↗	↗	↗	↷	↷	↷	↗
R	L	R	L	R	L	R	L

3-4

(Join hands. Arms up.)   (Arms move down and then up)

1	2	3	4	1	2	3	4
STAMP	—;	STAMP	—	STEP	STEP	MOVE	BACK;
						↓	↓
R		L		R	L	R	L

(Steps in place)

5-8   REPEAT "B" EXACTLY.

HOREHRONSKY CZARDAS

Slovakian Girls' Circle Dance
(Slovakia is the southeastern section of Czechoslovakia)

Pronounced Hora-ráhn-skee Char-dahsh

This dance was introduced by Anatol Joukowsky who had observed it in a town in Slovakia just prior to World War II. The name refers to the upper valley of the Hron River. Mr. Joukowsky says that this is a girls' spring ritual dance which somehow is related to wedding magic beliefs.

The dance starts slowly (the music has a haunting quality) and becomes more exciting. The last figure, which shows strong Hungarian influence, is marvelous.

This dance is included here with the permission of Anatol M. Joukowsky, San Francisco, California.

Record: Apon 2126

Formation: Circle.

Hands joined.

Free foot — R.

SEQUENCE		
Measures		
4/4		
1-4		Introduction — wait 16 counts.
1-24	**A** **Walk & Twist**	Walk and twist 6 times (at end free foot — L.)
2/4		
1-8		2 Box
9-12 **B**		1 Diagonal
13-16 **Side &**		1 Box
17-20 **Diagonal**		1 Diagonal
21-24		1 Box
1-24		REPEAT "B" EXACTLY.
1-8		8 Side steps
9-12 **C**		1 Diagonal
13-16 **Side &**		4 Side steps
17-20 **Diagonal**		1 Diagonal
21-24		4 Side steps
1-4		6 Open Ridas, then 4 runs CW
5-8 **D**		6 Open Ridas, then 4 runs CW
9-12 **Open**		1 Diagonal
13-16 **Rida &**		8 Open Ridas
17-20 **Diagonal**		1 Diagonal
21-23		6 Open Ridas, then

	1	&	2	&
24 **Ending**	SIDE ← L	CLOSE R	RISE on toes	HANDS up

Music 4/4 and 2/4

Steps:
Music 4/4

Measures

	(Face R)		(Face center)		(Face R)		(Face center)	
	1	2	3	4	1	2	3	4
1-2	WALK	WALK	SIDE	CLOSE;	WALK	WALK	SIDE	CLOSE;
	↗	↗	→		↗	↗	→	
	R	L	R	L	R	L	R	L

Walk & Twist

	(Toward center)		(Hands up)					
	1	2	3	4	1	2	3	4
3-4	STEP	TOUCH	STEP	TOUCH;	BACK	TWO	THREE	FOUR;
	↰	(Beside R)	↱	(Beside L)	↓	↓	↓	↓
	R	(L)	L	(R)	R	L	R	L

Music 2/4

Measures

1-4 Box

(Face center) (Bend and straighten knees on each count of "side, close")

1	2	1	2	1	2	1	&	2	&
SIDE	CLOSE;	FORWARD	CLOSE;	SIDE	CLOSE;	BACK-BACK-BACK-BACK;			
←	(Beside L)	↑	(Beside L)	←	(Beside L)	↓	↓	↓	↓
L	R	L	R	L	R	L - R - L - R			

1-4 Diagonal

(Face center) (Bend knees)

1	&	2	1	&	2	1	&	2	&	1	&	2	&
STEP-CLOSE-STEP;			STEP-CLOSE-STEP;			STEP-CLOSE		LEAP-CLOSE;		BACK-BACK-BACK-BACK;			
↖	↖	↓	↗	↗	↓	↗		↗		↓	↓	↓	↓
L - R - L			R - L - R			L	(R)	R	(L)	L - R - L - R			

1 Side Step

(L hip leads on "side" step)

(Face R)	(Face center)
1	2
SIDE	CLOSE;
←	
L	R

(This is similar to the first two counts of the BOX.)

1 Open Rida

(Face center)

1	&	2	&
SIDE-CROSS		SIDE-CROSS;	
←	↖	←	↖
L - R		L - R	

(Dance two rida steps to one measure.)

IBO

Nigeria, West Africa

Pronounced: Eé-bo — dance for a man and a woman.

For large groups — drum in center, then a circle of men and then a circle of women on outside.

This dance was introduced into this country by Annette Macdonald and Mary Joyce who did field research in 1966 in the Caribbean island of Carriacou. They collected many dances which are performed today by the descendents of the early slaves in the West Indies. "Ibo" is included here with their permission.

Ms. Macdonald says, "The dance is part of a collective complex, 16 to 18 in number, all of which make up "The Big Drum Dance." The Big Drum Dance consists of 'creole' dances and 'nation' dances; the creole dances are a product of acculturation in the new world (meaning some European influence), whereas the nation dances are said to be brought from West Africa — IBO is a nation dance, from the Ibo tribe in Nigeria.

"The Big Drum Dance is a traditional part of the ancestral cult ceremony. Carriacouans hold a Big Drum Dance on important occasions on which the blessing of the ancestors is desired, or as a sign of respect to ensure safety from the ancestors' disfavor. The dance is also done purely for pleasure."

Records: "IBO," Drumbeat Records 1001 B. (Introduction — slow drum beats and 27 counts of fast beating.)

"African Heritage Dances," Educational Activities Album, AR 36, Freeport, N.Y. 11520. (4 measure introduction.)

Music: 4/4. Women and men alternate dancing. While waiting, dancers keep beat by moving in place. They improvise movements or just keep the beat with the two-step.

VOCAL — Women Dance

Measures

1-2 **A Two-Step**

(Elbows bent, palms facing, hands cut downward across body in same direction as the two-step.)

1	&	2	3	&	4	1	&	2	3	&	4
STEP-CLOSE-STEP			STEP-CLOSE-STEP;			STEP-CLOSE-STEP			STEP-CLOSE-STEP;		
→		→	←		←	→		→	←		←
R* - L - R*			L* - R - L*			R* - L - R*			L* - R - L*		

*Hands cut down.

3-4 REPEAT "A" EXACTLY (8 two-steps in all).

5-6 **B Elbow Dip**

(Similar to Samba)

1	&	2	3	&	4	1	&	2	3	&	4
STEP-STEP-CLOSE			STEP-STEP-CLOSE;			STEP-STEP-CLOSE			STEP-STEP-CLOSE;		
↑	↓		↑	↓		↑	↓		↑	↓	
R - L - R			L - R - L			R - L - R			L - R - L		

Bend knee (Beside L) Bend knee (Beside R)

(Accent count "1")
(On count "1" the opposite elbow dips downward across body)

7-8 **C Turn & Dig**

(One complete left turn . . . .)   (In place — bend knee on each step)

1	2	3	4	1	2	3	4
STEP	STEP	STEP	STEP;	STEP	STEP	STEP	STEP;
↶	↶	↶	↶	(in place)	(in place)	(in place)	(in place)
R	L	R	L	R	L	R	L

DRUMS — Men Dance

1-2 **A Twirl Towel**

(Holding ends of scarf or towel with both hands — lean forward and twirl towel.)

1	&	2	3	&	4	1	&	2	1	&	4
STEP-CLOSE-STEP			STEP-CLOSE-STEP;			STEP-CLOSE-STEP			STEP-CLOSE-STEP;		
→		→	←		←	→		→	←		←
R - L - R			L - R - L			R - L - R			L - R - L		

3-4 REPEAT "A" EXACTLY (8 two-steps in all).

5-6 **B Stamps**

(Hold towel high with R hand. Flip it forward with each stamp.)

1	2	3	4	5	6	7	8
STAMP	STAMP	STAMP	STAMP	STAMP	STAMP	STAMP	STEP;
↑	↑	↑	↑	↑	↑	↑	↓
(R) (no wt)	(R)	(R)	(R)	(R)	(R)	(R)	R

(Keep weight on left foot during all the stamps.)

7-8 **C Kick Around and Jump**

(complete turn)

1	&	2	3	4	1	2	3	4
STEP-KICK-SPIN			LUMP	——;	JUMP	JUMP	JUMP	JUMP;
(in place) ↗ ↶		(in place)			(in place)	(in place)	(in place)	(in place)
		← →			← →	← →	← →	← →
L	R	Both	Both		Both	Both	Both	Both

References in Bibliograpy: 14 (Side B), 19 (p. 57).

IPHI NDILELA
South African

Pronounced Eēp-inn-dáy-lah.

Dance is an important part of the daily life of the people who live in the villages in South Africa. Dance is a very personal matter and it is used as a form of communicating one's inner feelings to the group. There are very few set-pattern dances in this area. Each dancer expresses himself by improvising as he dances.

Iphi Ndilela is a farewell song. Someone is leaving the village to find a new life and the villagers are dancing their goodbyes. They show their sadness at her leaving, but they also show through more exciting movements that they wish her luck.

The author learned this dance in 1969 from Odinga Lumumba, dancer and teacher of African dance. Mr. Lumumba has given his permission to include the dance here.

Record: Makeba, Reprise Records, RS-6310
Side 2, band 1

Or other African music with a good 4/4 beat

Formation: Circle of individual dancers — hands not joined.

Solo dancer in center.

Three basic steps are used in this dance.

	1	2	3	4
Basic #1	STEP	STEP	STEP	STEP;

Step on every beat. Either foot. Torso hangs relaxed, either slightly forward or low. Drop into the step. One or both shoulders drop with the stepping.

(Sideward movement — may face into circle or may face out)

	&	1	&	2	&	3	&	4
Basic #2	STEP	CLOSE	STEP	CLOSE	STEP	CLOSE	STEP	CLOSE;

This is like small galloping steps close to the floor.

Head is relaxed.

Arms hang completely relaxed.

(Move forward)

Basic #3

1	2
STEP (R heel comes off floor)	STEP (L heel comes off floor)
↑	↑
L	R

Knees and calves are kept <u>tight</u> together.

Torso is upright.

Arms hang loose.

The directions for this dance are simply suggestions because each dancer does what he wants to when he wants to do it.

Start with Basic #1. Move in a circle around the solo dancer. May do solo turn and then continue circling around soloist.

May change to Basic #2 or Basic #3 at any time.

Most of the time the dancers move around the soloist using one of the basics and changing from one to another of the basics at will.

This is an expressive dance performed by individuals.

JAMBO

Ghana, African-Individual Dance

Pronounced Jáhm-bo. (Means *"Hello"* in Swahili)

The research for this dance was done by Annette Macdonald during a trip to Africa in 1970. She has used typical dance movements of the people of Ghana and has arranged these movements for recreational dancing.

The dancers come into the village center to meet their friends and to dance with them on Saturday night.

African dancing is very vigorous and very enjoyable if you let yourself go. Let the shoulders and pelvic girdle be loose. Use large movements.

This dance is included with the permission of Annette Macdonald, California State University, San Jose, California.

Record: Malayisha (Reverse side of Pata Pata) Reprise Records 9732

Formation: Two concentric circles

(inner circle face out, outer circle face in).

SEQUENCE	
Opening — 4 lunges	
AA	Hip Twist
BB	Knee Lift
CC	3s
AA	Hip Twist
BB	Knee Lift
CC	3s
AA	Hip Twist
BB	Knee Lift
CC	3s — move off

Music 4/4

Measures

1-7½   Introduction — count "<u>1</u>, 2, 3, 4, <u>2</u>, 2, 3, 4, ... <u>7</u>, 2, 3, 4, <u>8</u>, <u>2</u> <u>LUNGE</u>."
        May use this time to get into formation with TOUCH STEP, TOUCH STEP, etc., or may
        start in concentric circles and merely keep the beat with body movements and finger
        snaps.

Opening
Statement   ⎧ (2 concentric circles — one circle faces the other)
             ⎪ (Arms out to sides)

1	2	3	4	1	2	3	4
LUNGE	——	NOD	——;	NOD	——	NOD	——;

1-2 **Greet**   LUNGE ↗ R   NOD ↗   NOD ↑   NOD ↗
    Friends ⎨ & nod to   to "1"   to   to
             ⎪   friend   again   friend   "1"
             ⎩   "1"   "2"

3-8   Dance OPENING 3 more times. Four lunges in all (to R, to L, to R, to L).
       Alternate the lunges to "2," to "1," to "2."
       Big arm circle when changing.

        ⎧ (3 slow ones and 2 quick ones)
        ⎪ (All dancers move to own R. Smile at many friends.)

1	2	3	4	1	2	3	4	1	2	3	4	1	2	3	4
SIDE	——	CLOSE	——;	SIDE	——	CLOSE	——;	SIDE	——	CLOSE	——;	SIDE	CLOSE	SIDE	CLOSE;

A   → (Beside R)   →   →   →   →
1-4 **Hip**
    Twist ⎨ R   L   R   L   R   L   R   L   R   L
        ⎪ (Same shoulder as moving foot twists forward on each action)
        ⎩ (Big arm movements. Do what feels natural.)

5-8   REPEAT "A" EXACTLY.

Go on to next page

(On each knee lift, throw head back. Use big arm movements.)

	1	2	3	4	1	2	3	4
1-2	LIFT	LOWER	LIFT	STEP;	LIFT	LOWER	LIFT	STEP;
	(R)	(R)	(R)	R	(L)	(L)	(L)	L
	knee		knee	(Beside L)	knee		knee	(Beside R)

B Knee Lifts

(Land in forward stride position.)
(R foot back. Arms overhead.)

	1	2	3	4	1	2	3	4
3-4	LIFT	LOWER	LIFT	STEP;	JUMP	——	——	——;
	(R)	(R)	(R)	R	L↑			
				(Beside L)	R↓			

5-8 **B**   REPEAT "B" EXACTLY, but on JUMP the L foot is back and the R foot is forward.

(Four 3s in place. Big arm movements.)

	1	&	2	3	&	4	1	&	2	3	&	4
1-2	STEP-STEP-STEP			STEP-STEP-STEP;			STEP-STEP-STEP			STEP-STEP-STEP;		
	L - R - L			R - L - R			L - R - L			R - L - R		
		(clap)			(clap)			(clap)			(clap)	

C 3s

(Move forward — through other circle)   (Turn L to face other circle)

	1	&	2	1	&	4	1	2	3	4
3-4	STEP-STEP-STEP			STEP-STEP-STEP			STEP	KICK	LUMP	——;
	↑ ↑ ↑			↑ ↑ ↑			↑			
	L - R - L			R - L - R			L	(R)	Both	
		(clap)			(clap)			↙	←→	
								(Knees bent.		
								Arms out.)		

5-8   **C**   REPEAT "C." Finish in original circle.

Repeat dance from "A." The opening statement is done only once.

JESUCITA EN CHIHUAHUA

Mexican Couple Dance

Pronounced Hay-soo-sée-tah en Chee-wáh-wah

This dance was arranged by Alura Flores de Angeles for recreational dancing and is included here with her permission. It uses typical dance steps from the northern part of Mexico. It is a very enjoyable dance in that it gives the dancer the Mexican flavor without having to do the difficult heel work which is found in many Mexican dances.

The author learned this dance at the Indianapolis International Folk Dance Workshop in 1973.

Records: Peerless 3248 (45)

National 4511 (45)

Jessie Polka, Longhorn Records 201

Or any <u>fast</u> Jessie Polka Square record which has 11 sixteen-measure phrases.

If not, make adjustments by adding another "A" at end.

Formation: Couples in varsovienne position.

Face counterclockwise (LOD).

Both use same foot — exceptions are indicated.

Free foot — R.

Music 2/4

Measures

1-4		Introduction — wait (may be different on different records).

1-16   **A Two-Step**

(Varsovienne position)
(16 modified two-steps in all. Move into LOD)

1	&	2	&		1	&	2	&	
STEP-STEP-STEP-SCUFF;					STEP-STEP-STEP-SCUFF;				Continue
↑	↑	↑	HEEL		↑	↑	↑	HEEL	
R -	L -	R	(L)		L -	R -	L	(R)	

(On last two measures, without dropping hands, turn individually to own R. She remains on outside of circle.)

1-16   **A** REPEAT "A" moving into <u>reverse</u> LOD. Turn L on last 2 measures.

Go on to next page

(Into LOD)   (Drop L hands)
                                                    (She makes 2 turns to her R)

1-4 **B Girl Turns** {

1	2	1	2	1	2	1	2
WALK	WALK;	WALK	WALK;	STEP	STEP;	STEP	STEP;
↑	↑	↑	↑	↷	↶	↷	↶
R	L	R	L	R	L	R	L

(He continues walking forward)

5-16   DANCE "B" three <u>more</u> times.

1-16 **A**   DANCE "A" forward into LOD. No turn.

1-2 **C Wheel** {

(Side by side — his R arm around her waist, her arms hang down.)
(Wheel to R — as a couple — use 16 measures for one complete turn.)

1	2	1	2
STAMP	CLOSE;	BACK	CLOSE;	(This is similar to a slow Tcherkessia.)
↑		↓	
R	L	R	L

3-16   Contine with wheeling.

1-16 **C**   REPEAT "C" making a second wheel around.

1-4 **D Slides** {

(Closed position — joined hands point to center)
(She uses other foot)   (Slide to center of circle)

1	2	1	2	1	&	2	&	1	&	2
HEEL	TOE;	HEEL	TOE;	SIDE-CLOSE		SIDE-CLOSE		SIDE-CLOSE		SIDE;
←··	··→	←··	··→	←		←		←		←
(L)	(L)	(L)	(L)	L - R		L - R		L - R		L

(Hopping on R)

5-8   DANCE "D" with opposite footwork — slide toward wall.

9-12   DANCE "D" sliding in toward center.

13-16   DANCE "D" sliding toward wall.

1-16	C	Wheeling — side by side — go only once around.
1-16	A	Two-step forward (heel scuff).
1-16	B	Girl turns.

1   **E**
      Merengue

(Closed position — his back to center)
(Move sidewards into LOD. She uses other foot.)

	1	2
	SIDE	CLOSE; When stepping with a bent knee, force the opposite hip up.
	←	
	L	R
	(With	(With
	bent	bent
	knee)	knee)

2-16   DANCE "E" 15 <u>more</u> times — Ole!

SEQUENCE
A Two-steps LOD
A Two-steps RLOD
B Girl Turns
A Two-steps LOD
C Wheeling
C Wheeling
D Heel-toe Slide
C Wheeling
A Two-steps LOD
B Girl Turns
E Merengue

JUGO

East Europe circle dance

Pronounced Yóo - go

Huig Hofman, noted authority on European folk dancing, discovered this dance in a Displaced Persons Camp at the end of World War II. Because of the language barrier, he could not determine the name of the country of origin. The writer learned the dance from Dr. Bernard Kaimen, a participant at the Blue Star Israeli Folk Dance Camp in 1966.

The change of pace makes this a delightful dance.

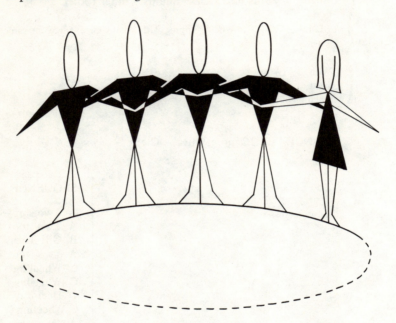

Record: Roumanian Hora — Folkraft F 010-45.

Folkraft 337-010.

Formation: Circle, no partners.

Front baskethold — R hand over. Beginners use simple hand hold.

Free foot — R.

Music 4/4

Measures

1-2   Introduction

A Schottische

	(Face R)				(Face L)			
	1	2	3	4				
	STEP	STEP	STEP	HOP;	STEP	STEP	STEP	HOP;
	↗	↗	↗		↖	↖	↖	
	R	L	R	R	L	R	L	L

1-2

3-8   DANCE "A" THREE MORE TIMES (8 schottisches in all)

B Toe-Taps

	(Face center)							
	1	2	3	4	1	2	3	4
	SIDE	———;	CLOSE	———;	TAP	TAP	TOUCH	———;
	→				↑	⋅⋅→	(beside L)	
	R		L		R	R	R	

1-2

3-8   DANCE "B" THREE MORE TIMES

C Rocking

	(Face center)							
	1	2	3	4	1	2	3	4
	LEAP	LEAP	LEAP	LEAP;	LEAP	LEAP	LEAP	LEAP;
	↖	↓	↖	↓	↖	↓	↖	↓
	R	L	R	L	R	L	R	L

1-2

(Circle moves to the left)

3-8   DANCE "C" THREE MORE TIMES

Style — A easy and natural,
          B sharp and exact,
          C circle really moves.

For each dance:

1. Say the capitalized words.
2. Do what you say
3. In the direction of the arrow
4. With the indicated foot.

Reference in Bibliography: 20 (p. 21).

KALVELIS

Little Blacksmith
Lithuanian circle dance

Pronounced Cal-vále-iss

　　This dance, which is a favorite of Americans and Lithuanians, was introduced in this country by
V. F. Beliajus, one of the outstanding folk dance authorities and editor of *Viltis*, the folklore magazine.
The dance is considered an occupational dance of the smithy. The handclapping suggests the striking
of the hammer on the anvil. The dance is gay and playful.

　　This dance was arranged from a dance description in *Merrily Dance* by V. F. Beliajus and reproduced
here with the author's permission.

Records: Folkraft 1051

　　　　　Folk Dancer 1016

Formation: Couples in a single circle.

　　　　　Woman on R of man.

　　　　　All join hands.

　　　　　All use same foot. Free foot — R.

STYLE — Lithuanian polkas are done with almost
no hop. The men dance more vigorously
than the women.

Music 2/4

Measures

1-2		Introduction (count 4 beats)

1-8   **A**   **Circle**

POLKA   TO   RIGHT (7 of them)
          1   &   2
STAMP - STAMP - STAMP
     L - R - L

1-8

POLKA   TO   LEFT (7 of them)
          1   &   2
STAMP - STAMP - STAMP
     L - R - L

1-4   **X**   **CHORUS**

(Face partner. Clap own hands)   (Hook R elbows)
 1   2   1   2   1   2   1   2
CLAP, CLAP; CLAP, CLAP;   SKIP, SKIP; SKIP, SKIP;

R hand | L | R | L
on top, | on top, | on top, | on top

5-8

(Face partner)   (Hook L elbows)
CLAP, CLAP; CLAP, CLAP;   SKIP, SKIP; SKIP, SKIP;

1-8   REPEAT CLAPPING AND ELBOW SWINGS

1-4   **B**   **TO**   **CENTER**

(Face center — men stand still)   (Turn to face partner)
WOMEN POLKA IN   (3)   STAMP - STAMP - STAMP

5-8

WOMEN POLKA OUT   (3)   STAMP - STAMP - STAMP

1-4

                          (Turn to face partner)
MEN   POLKA IN   (3)   STAMP - STAMP - STAMP

5-8

MEN   POLKA OUT   (3)   STAMP - STAMP - STAMP

1-16   **X**   REPEAT CHORUS (Claps and elbow swings)

1-16   **C**   **GRAND**   **R & L**

(Face partner and join R hands to start — men go CCW)
  POLKAS   (16)

Keep new partner on last polka.

1-16   **X**   REPEAT CHORUS WITH NEW PARTNER (Claps and elbow swings)

SEQUENCE: A-X-B-X-C-X-A-X-B-X-C-X-A

References in Bibliography: 1 (p. 5), 13 (p. 144), 15 (p. 230), 20 (p. 90).

Kalvelis   77

KARAGOUNA

Greek Line Dance

Pronounced Kair-ah-góo-nah

Because this Greek dance is very satisfying in movement and in music it has become a favorite of the college students. They especially enjoy the contrasting movements of the walks and the hip twists. The last part of the dance, the Syrtos, (the Greeks call this part the Kalamatianos) which is quite fast offers a delightful change of pace.

Styling: All of the steps are taken with a bouncing action of the supporting knee.

Although there are many recordings for the Karagouna dance, some of them do not include the fast part. The leader on the right end of the line should make whatever adjustments are necessary.

Record: Greek Dance Party, Tikva T-131, Side A, Band 4.

            Other suggested recordings: Greek Folk Dances, Folkraft LP-3.

                                             Picnic in Greece, OL 24-13.

Formation: Line or broken circle. Leader on right end.

              Joined hands are shoulder high.

              Free foot − R.

              Line of direction (LOD) is counterclockwise.

Note: It is easier to learn this dance if the Syrto dance on page 144 has been mastered. The Syrto may be done with or without the hop.

Music 2/4

Measures

1-8   Introduction — wait 16 counts.

		(Face to R)			(Face Center)				
		1	2	1	2	ah - 1	2	1	2
1-4 | **A** **Slow** **Walk &** **Point** | { | WALK ↗ R | WALK; ↗ L | WALK ↗ R | POINT; ↑⋮ (L) | HOP-STEP ↓ R - L | POINT; ↘⋱ (R) | POINT; ⋰↗ (R) | POINT; ↘⋱ (R) |

5-16   REPEAT "A" THREE MORE TIMES

		1	2	1	2	1	2	1	2
1-4 | **B*** **Hip** **Twist** | { | SIDE → R | CLOSE; L | SIDE → R | CLOSE; L | SIDE → R | CLOSE; L | SIDE → R | CLOSE; L |

(Face center — while hopping, hold the free leg across in front)

		1	2	&	1	2	1	2	&	1	2
5-8 | **C** **Hop-Hop** | { | POINT ⋰↗ (R) | HOP-HOP; L - L | STEP ↖ R | TOUCH; ←⋯ (L) | POINT ↖⋰ (L) | HOP-HOP; R - R | STEP ↗ L | TOUCH; ⋯→ (R) |

(Face right . . . .)(Face center . . . .)

		1	2	&	1	2	&	1	2	&	1	2	&
9-12 | **D** **Fast** **Syrto** | { | STEP ↗ R | STEP-STEP; ↗ ↗ L - R | FRONT ↗ L | STEP-STEP; ↗ ↗ R - L | SIDE → R | OVER-BACK ↗ L - R | SIDE ← L | OVER-BACK; ↖ ↘ R - L |

13-16   REPEAT "D" EXACTLY.

*On the "side" step, twist the body to face left. Let the hip lead. On the "close" face the center.

NOTE: If recording does not include the fast music, omit "D" but repeat "B" and "C."

References in Bibliography: 13 (p. 42), 18 (p. 99).

KARAPYET

Russian couple dance

Pronounced Kah-ráh-pee-yet.

This dance, which is sometimes called the Russian Two-Step, was introduced in this country by Michael Herman, the well-known folk dance authority and director of Folk Dance House in New York City. The dance is reproduced here with Mr. Herman's permission.

Just as the people in Indiana are jokingly called Hoosiers, the people who lived in the Caucasus were jokingly called Karapyets. We can assume that the dance originated in that particular part of Russia. The dance was popular in the late 1800s and the early 1900s. It was done by city people at weddings and other celebrations. The dance is an exciting dance of the ballroom type. The basic step, Russian Two-Step, is very smooth and gives the feeling of gliding.

Records: Folk Dancer MH 1058

Folkraft 1169

Formation: Closed social dance position.

Double circle — Man's back to center.

Directions are for man.

Woman uses <u>other</u> foot.

Line of direction (LOD) is counterclockwise (CCW).

Free foot — Man's L, woman's R.

For each dance:

1. Say the capitalized words.
2. Do what you say
3. In the direction of the arrow
4. With the indicated foot.

Music 2/4

Measures

Introduction — 3 chords and a cymbal clash.

<table>
<tr><td>1-4</td><td>**A**
Toe</td><td colspan="8">
1   2   1   2   1   2   1   2
TOUCH ———; TOUCH ———; WALK WALK; WALK ———;
←··   (beside R)   ↖   ↖   ↖
(L)   (L)   L   R   L
</td></tr>
</table>

(Keep closed position but look RLOD)(Both move forward in RLOD)

1	2	1	2	1	2	1	2
TOUCH ———;		TOUCH ———;		WALK	WALK;	WALK ———;	
··→		(beside L)		↗	↗	↗	
(R)		(R)		R	L	R	

5-8

NOTE: While doing the "Touch" rise on toe of supporting foot.

1-4   **B**
Russian
Two-
Steps

(Forward in LOD)   (Drop hands - solo turn)
(Inside hands joined)   (Progress in LOD)
(Stretch free arm) (Bend free arm) (One complete turn, woman to R)

1	&	2	1	&	2	1	&	2	1	&	2
LEAP-RUN-RUN;			LEAP-RUN-RUN;			LEAP-RUN-RUN;			LEAP-RUN-RUN;		
↑	↑	↑	↑	↑	↑	↖			↘		
L	-	R - L	R	-	L - R	L	- R -	L	R	- L -	R

("B" is four Russian 2-steps, two of them are forward, turning slightly away from partner and then slightly toward partner. Then two are turning individually while progressing in the line of direction.)

5-8   REPEAT "B" EXACTLY.

(Join inside hands. <u>Keep them joined</u> until beginning of final turn.)

(Both face LOD)   (Half turn   (Half turn
                     toward   toward
                     partner)   partner)

1-4   **C**

1	2	1	2	1	2	1	2
WALK	WALK;	WALK	PIVOT;	WALK	WALK;	WALK	PIVOT;
↑	↑	↑	↷	↗	↗	↗	↶
L	R	L	L	R	L	R	R

(Closed position)
(One complete turn CW. . . . . . .)
(Progress CCW)

1	&	2	1	&	2	1	&	2	1	&	2
LEAP-RUN-RUN;			LEAP-RUN-RUN;			STEP-CLOSE-STEP;			STEP-CLOSE-STEP;		
↑	↑	↑	↑	↑	↑	←		←	→		→
L	-	R - L	R	-	L - R	L	- R -	L	R	- L -	R

5-8

References in Bibliography: 15 (p. 102), 22 (p. 188).

KOHONOTCHKA

Russian couple dance

Pronounced Koh-háh-notch-kah

    This is a Russian dance which was popular in the ballrooms of Russia during the late 1800s and early 1900s. It should have a smooth flowing feeling.

Record: Folk Dancer MH 1058.

Formation: Couples facing CCW.

                Inside hands joined.

                Other arm bent with elbow out to side, hand in front of chest.

                Directions are for man. Woman does reverse.

                Free foot — Man's L, woman's R.

For each dance:

1. **Say the capitalized words.**
2. **Do what you say**
3. **In the direction of the arrow**
4. **With the indicated foot.**

Music 2/4

Measures

1-4   Introduction

1-4   **A**   (Stretch free arm)   (Bend free arm)   (Drop hands — one complete solo turn)
      Russian   (Progress in LOD — woman turns R)
      Two-Steps   1   &   2   1   &   2   1   &   2   1   &   2

LEAP-RUN-RUN;   LEAP-RUN-RUN;   LEAP-RUN-RUN;   LEAP-RUN-RUN;

L - R - L   R - L - R   L - R - L   R - L - R

5-8   REPEAT "A" EXACTLY.

1-4   **B**   1   2   1   2   1   &   2   1   &   2
      Varsovienne   STEP   TOUCH; STEP   TOUCH;   LEAP-RUN-RUN;   LEAP-RUN-RUN;
      Position   (Beside L)   (Beside R)
                  L   (R)   R   (L)   L - R - L   R - L - R

5-8   REPEAT "B" EXACTLY.

C

1-4   (Face partner)   (Move away from partner)   (Man to center — woman to wall)
          1   2   1   &   2   1   &   2   1   &   2
         CLAP   CLAP;   LEAP-RUN-RUN;   LEAP-RUN-RUN;   LEAP-RUN-RUN;
         (own)   (own)   L - R - L   R - L - R   L - R - L

5-8   (Pass left shoulders)
         1   2   1   &   2   1   &   2   1   &   2
         CLAP   CLAP;   LEAP-RUN-RUN;   LEAP-RUN-RUN;   LEAP-RUN-RUN;
         (own)   (own)   L - R - L   R - L - R   L - R - L

1-4   (Pass left shoulders)
         1   2   1   &   2   1   &   2   1   &   2
         CLAP   CLAP;   LEAP-RUN-RUN;   LEAP-RUN-RUN;   LEAP-RUN-RUN;
         (own)   (own)   L - R - L   R - L - R   L - R - L

5-8   (Face LOD)   (Progress in LOD)
                                    (Individual turn — woman turns R)
         1   2   1   2   1   &   2   1   &   2
         CLAP   CLAP;   ___   ___;   LEAP-RUN-RUN   LEAP-RUN-RUN;
         (own)   (own)   (Pause)   L - R - L   R - L - R

References in Bibliography: 11 (p. 224), 12 (p. 61), 15 (p. 104).

KOROBUSHKA

Peddler's Pack
Russian couple dance

Pronounced Kuh-rŏb-esh-kah

   This dance was brought to the United States in the early 1900s by Russian immigrants. Many variations have developed over the years and different sections of our country use different styles. It is especially enjoyable when danced as a mixer.

Record: Folkraft 1170.

Folk Dancer M H 1059.

Imperial 1022.

Kismet 106.

World of Fun M 108.

Formation: Double circle of partners.

Man's back to center.

Both hands joined.

Both use same foot.

Free foot — R.

84

Music 4/4

Measures

1-2   Introduction

1-2	**A** **Schottische** **and** **Across-** **Apart-** **Together**	(Both hands joined) SCHOTTISCHE 2 3 HOP; SCHOTTISCHE 2 3 HOP; (toward ↑ wall) ↑ ↑ (toward ↓ center) ↓ ↓ R L R R L R L L

3-4		1 2 3 4
		SCHOTTISCHE 2 3 HOP; TOUCH TOUCH TOGETHER - - - - ;
		(toward ↑ wall) ↑ ↑
		       R L R R (L) (L) Both
		                                    (Hop R) (Hop R)

1-2	**Schottische**
	
	B
		(Drop hands)
		(Each move to own R — smile at next person) (Return to partner)
		SCHOTTISCHE 2 3 HOP; SCHOTTISCHE 2 3 HOP:
		        ↗ ↗ ↗ ↖ ↖ ↖
		       R L R R L R L

3-4	**Balance**	(With original partner) (Drop M's L hand, W's R)
		(Join both hands) (Change sides with ptnr) (Face partner)
		     1 2 3 4 4
		   STEP HOP BACK HOP; WALK 2 3
		                     ↓ ↑ ↑ ↑ ↑
		    R R L L R L R L
		                                  (She turns L under joined hands)

1-4   REPEAT "B" EXACTLY. (From partner's original position — end in own original position.)

Variation — some groups prefer more action.

     In part "B" measure 1-2, turn to R a complete solo turn on first schottische and to left a full solo turn on second schottische.

     To do this as a mixer: **Do "B" and repeat "B."** Then on the very last three-step-turn to the left; do not move to the left. Do the turn in place and you will do the balance forward and back and change sides with a new partner.

References in Bibliography: 2 (p. 59), 11 (p. 225), 15 (p. 91), 16 (p. 165), 22 (p. 187)

KUJAWIAK #1 ADA'S

Polish Couple Dance

Pronounced Koo-yáh-vee-ack

This dance was arranged by Ada Dziewanowska, one of the outstanding specialists in Polish dancing, and is included here with her permission. The Kujawiak is one of the basic types of dances of Poland along with the Krakowiak, the Mazur, the Polonaise, and others. The Kujawiak is always done to a three beat and is characteristically walking and circling with a partner. The movement should be smooth, graceful, and fluid.

Record: "Farewell To My Country," MUZA LP XL0203, side A, band 3
(On the Willow Leaf)

Formation: Partners side by side.

Face line of direction CCW.

Hold inside hand.

Directions are for man.

She uses other foot.

Free foot — his L, her R.

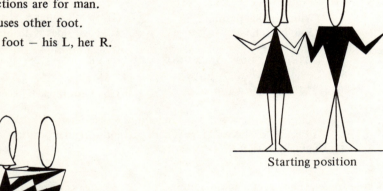

Starting position

Position at end of measure 4

Position for "C"

Music 3/4

1-4   Introduction — wait. May balance as in Interlude.

A
Into
LOD

1-4

(Hold inside hand. Face LOD.) (SHE starts R foot.)   (She moves in front and faces him.)
(Wave free arm forward and back at shlder height)   (He steps in place.)

1	2	3	1	2	3	1	2	3	1	2	3
WALK	WALK	WALK;	WALK	WALK	WALK;	WALK	WALK	WALK;	STEP	STEP	STEP;
L	R	L	R	L	R	L	R	L	R	L	R

5-8

(Shoulder-waist position.)
(She moves backward into LOD.)   (Both bend to L)

1	2	3	1	2	3	1	2	3	1	2	3
WALK	WALK	WALK;	WALK	WALK	WALK;	WALK	WALK	WALK;	BEND —		STRAIGHTEN
									KNEES		KNEES
L	R	L	R	L	R	L	R	L	Both		Both

B
Hips
Adjacent

9-12

(R hips adjacent) (Move CW around partner)
(Keep shoulder-waist postion)

1	2	3	1	2	3	1	2	3	1	2	3
WALK	WALK	WALK;	WALK	WALK	WALK;	WALK	WALK	WALK;	STAMP	STAMP	—;
L	R	L	R	L	R	L	R	L	R	L	

13-16 **B**   REPEAT "B" with L hips adjacent. Move CCW around partner.
Start with free foot.

1-16 **ABB**   REPEAT FROM BEGINNING.

C

1-4 **Walk**

(His R arm around her waist, her L hand on his shoulder.) (Only man slaps thigh-hi.) *
(Move into LOD. Outside fist on hip.)   (He steps in front
(Slightly   (Outside elbows touch)   of her.)
Back to back.)   (Face to face.)   (Back to back.)   (She moves backward
     L, R, L.)

WALK	WALK	WALK;	WALK	WALK	WALK;	WALK	WALK	WALK;	WALK	HIT	HIT;
										THIGH	THIGH
L	R	L	R	L	R	L	R	L	R	(L)	(L)

(with L hand)

She
Backs
Up

5-8

(Facing partner. Move CW in place. She moves backward.)

1	2	3	1	2	3	1	2	3	1	2	3
WALK	WALK	WALK;	WALK	WALK	WALK;	WALK	WALK	WALK;	STAMP	STAMP	—;
L	R	L	R	L	R	L	R	L	R	(L)	

(no wt.)

9-16 **C**   REPEAT "C" EXACTLY. Note: His R arm is around her waist during <u>all</u> of "C."

           1   2   3   1 2 3   1 2 3   1 2 3

Interlude — join both hands. Balance away; together; away; together;

     REPEAT DANCE FROM BEGINNING.

*Like slapping the thigh while on horseback.

LAKODALMI TANC

Hungarian wedding dance — girls only

Pronounced Lack-ah-dáhl-mee Tahns

This dance is based on research done by Andor Czompo in Hungary. It is a ceremonial dance which the bride's friends perform just prior to removing the bridal headdress. The dancers sing the accompaniment and carry a white handkerchief in the right hand. The dance is softly feminine and lyrical yet solemn. Mr. Czompo* suggests that the dancers learn the melody and hum it as they dance without any accompaniment. Thus the original flavor of the dance will be retained.

This dance is arranged from a description by Andor and Ann I. Czompo, *Hungarian Dances,* and reproduced here by permission of Andor Czompo.

Record: Crossroad label 4002.

Formation: Front baskethold.

R hand on top.

Hold large white handkerchief in R hand.

Free foot — R.

---

*Andor Czompo, Hungarian Dance authority now living in Homer, New York.

88

Music 3/8

Measures

1-4   Introduction — wait.

	(Face center) (Slow steps)					
	1	2	3	1	2	3
A **Slow** **In** **& Out**	IN ↑ R	——	——;	OUT ↓ L	——	——;
1-4	1	2	3	1	2	3
	SIDE → R	——	——;	CLOSE beside R L	——	——:

5-16   Do "A" 3 more times.

	(Face to right)					
	1	2	3	1	2	3
B **Slow** **To** **R**	STEP ↗ R	——	——;	STEP ↗ L	——	——;
1-4	1	2	3	1	2	3
	STEP ↗ R	——	——;	BACK ↙ L	——	——;

5-12   Do "B" 2 more times.

	(Face center)					
	1	2	3	1	2	3
B **Break**	SIDE → R	——	BACK; ↘ L	FRONT ↖ R	——	——;
13-16	1	2	3	1	2	3
	SIDE ← L	——	BACK; ↙ R	FRONT ↗ L	——	——;

Go on to next page

Music 2/4

		1	2		1	2
		FRONT	SIDE;		BACK	SIDE;
		↖	←		↙	←
		R	L		R	L

1-4

	1	2		1	2
	FRONT	SIDE;		BACK	SIDE:
	↖	←		↙	←
	R	L		R	L

**C
Grapevine
and
Turn**

(One complete solo R turn in place)
(Drop hands — let R arm lead)

1	2		1	2
TURN	TWO;		THREE	FOUR;
↗				
R	L		R	L

5-8

(Face center — join hands in baskethold)

1	2	1	2
SIDE	TOUCH;	SIDE	TOUCH;
→	(beside R)	←	(beside L)
R	(L)	L	(R)

9-32   Do "C" 3 <u>more</u> times.

Music 3/8

Measures

**D
Sway
and
Cross**

(Sway to R)

1	2	3		1	2	3
SIDE	——	——;		SIDE		CROSS ;
→				←		↖
R				L		R

(Sway to L)

1	2	3		1	2	3
SIDE		CROSS ;		SIDE	——	——;
←		↖		←		
L		R		L		

1-4

5-16   Do "D" 3 <u>more</u> times.

1-4 **E Little Grapevine**

(Face to R)

1	2	3		1	2	3
STEP	——	——;		STEP	——	——;
↗				↗		
R				L		

(Face center)
(Flowing grapevine)

1	2	3	1	2	3
SIDE		BACK;	SIDE		FRONT;
→		↘	→		↗
R		L	R		L

5-16 Do "E" 3 <u>more</u> times.

Music 2/4

1-4 **F Slow Grapevine and Finale**

(Face center)

1	2	1	2	1	2	1	2
FRONT	SIDE;	BACK	SIDE;	FRONT	SIDE;	BACK	SIDE;
↖	←	↙	←	↖	←	↙	←
R	L	R	L	R	L	R	L

(Drop hands)
(Solo turn in place. . . . . . .)   (Front baskethold)

TURN	TWO;	THREE	FOUR;	SIDE	BEHIND	SIDE	CLOSE;
↗				→	↘	→	and
R	L	R	L	R	L	R	bow

(Bend fwd from waist)

Reference in Bibliography: 3 (p. 52).

LAZ BAR
Armenian line dance

Pronounced Lahz Bar

"Bar" means dance.

   This very simple Armenian dance has a hypnotic effect on the dancer. The longer you dance it the more you enjoy it. The author learned this from Nancy Linson who danced it at the Kentucky Dance Institute in 1967.

Records: Hye Dughak, Rendezvous in Armenia, Roulette R 25230

   The Country Dance, Seventh Veil Lp, Kapp KL 1090

Formation: Open circle.

   Hands joined, little fingers interlocked (R palm up, L palm down).

   Hands at shoulder height.

   Free foot — R.

Music 2/4

Measures

1-8   Introduction

1-2	**A Four Two-Steps Side to Side**	(Swing hands to R) 1 & 2 STEP - CLOSE - STEP; → → R - L - R (Swing hands to L) 1 & 2 STEP - CLOSE - STEP; ← ← L - R - L

1-2 **A Four Two-Steps Side to Side**

(Swing hands to R)   (Swing hands to L)
1   &   2   1   &   2
STEP - CLOSE -STEP;   STEP - CLOSE - STEP;
→   →   ←   ←
R   -   L   -   R   L   -   R   -   L

3-4
1   &   2   1   &   2
STEP - CLOSE - STEP;   STEP - CLOSE - STEP;
→   →   ←   ←
R   -   L   -   R   L   -   R   -   L

5-6 **B Two-Step and Cross**

(Swing hands up)   (Swing hands down)
1   &   2   1   &   2
STEP - CLOSE - STEP;   STEP - CLOSE - STEP;
↑   ↑   ↓   ↓
R   -   L   -   R   L   -   R   -   L

7-8
1   2   1   2
(Hands up)   (Hands down)   (Hands up)   (Hands down)
(Lean back)   (Lean fwd)   (Lean back)   (Lean fwd)
SIDE   CROSS;   SIDE   CROSS;
→   ↗   →   ↗
R   L   R   L

For each dance:

1. Say the capitalized words.
2. Do what you say
3. In the direction of the arrow
4. With the indicated foot.

Reference in Bibliography: 23 (June 1967, p. 18).

LITTLE MAN IN A FIX

Danish mixer by couples

    This dance was brought to our country by various Danish Folk Dance Societies. It is a joyful dance and still very popular.

    The fun part of the dance is the wheel. If the man is not quick enough to get another couple for the wheel, he and his partner wait in the center of the room. She is so disgusted with him she scolds him and that makes him "The Little Man in a Fix."

Record: Folk Dancer MH 1054

Formation: Two couples in wheel formation.

                Partners side by side facing same direction.

                Two men link L elbows.

                Man's L hand joined to other woman's L hand behind her partner's back.

                Man's R arm around partner's waist.

                Free foot — Man's L, woman's R.

Music 3/4

Measures

3 chords		Introduction
1-8	A	WHEEL – One <u>long</u> phrase (If you must count, it's 24)
		(Run, stressing count "1" of each measure)
		(Hands are joined behind backs)
1-8	B	BASKET – One long phrase – continue running
		(Spread out. Hold nearest hands throughout "B." Men make arch with joined L hands. Pull partner under arch. Ladies half turn to left and join R hands above men's joined hands.)
	C	TYROLEAN WALTZ* (16 measures) (Keep holding ptnr's hand. Drop opposite's hand)
1-4		4 forward waltzes side by side
5-8		4 turning waltzes in closed position
1-4		4 forward waltzes side by side
5-8		4 turning waltzes in closed position

To repeat dance, find a new couple to dance with. Men link L elbows for the wheel.

The odd couple stands in center of room until part "C."

References in Bibliography: 11 (p. 182), 15 (p. 118).

*See page 154 for Tyrolean Waltz.

MAKAZICE

Serbian line dance

Pronounced Mah-kah-zée-tsee.

This dance was introduced in this country in 1954 by Richard Crum, noted authority on Balkan dancing, and is included here with his permission. The first version presented here is the version which Richard Crum learned in Serbia. The second version of "B" was taught to the author by Norman Tischler, a graduate student at Ball State University in 1968.

The name of the dance means "Scissors" and it is derived from part "B."

Record: Folk Dancer MH 45-3023

Formation: Line or open circle.

Joined hands are low.

Leader at R end.

Free foot — R.

Music 4/4

Measures

1-8   Introduction — let the music play through the dance one time. Listen for the "scissors" part.

<table>
<tr><td>1-2</td><td rowspan="2">**A**
Side</td><td colspan="8">

1	2	3	4	5	6	7	8
SIDE	BEHIND	SIDE	BEHIND;	SIDE	BEHIND	SIDE	____ ;
→	↘	→	↘	→	↘	→	
R	L	R	L	R	L	R	

</td></tr>
<tr><td>3-4</td><td colspan="8">

1	2	3	4	1	2	3	4
SIDE	BEHIND	SIDE	BEHIND;	SIDE	BEHIND	SIDE	____ ;
←	↙	←	↙	←	↙	←	
L	R	L	R	L	R	L	

</td></tr>
</table>

5-6   **B**
(Scissors)

1	2	3	4	5	6	7	8
STEP	____	CROSS	____ ;	PULL	____	JUMP	____ ;
↑		↗		↓ ↓		(In pl)	
R		L		Both		Both	

You can hear this "scissors" plainly in the music.

7-8   REPEAT "B" EXACTLY.

VARIATION

5-6   **B**
(Scissors)

1	2	3	4	5	6	7	8
STEP	____	CROSS	____ ;	PULL	OUT	IN	____ ;
↑		↗		↓ ↓	↙ ↘	↘ ↙	
R		L		Both	Both	Both	

"Scissors"

7-8   REPEAT "B" EXACTLY.

For each dance:

1. **Say the capitalized words.**
2. **Do what you say**
3. **In the direction of the arrow**
4. **With the indicated foot.**

MA NAVU

Israeli circle dance

Pronounced Mah Nah-vóo

    This dance was choreographed by Raya Spivak and the music was written by Josef Spivak. It is a lovely quiet dance which uses the undulating quality of the Yemenite step. The author was introduced to the dance by Fred Berk, noted Israeli dance authority, in 1966 at the Blue Star Israeli Folk Dance Camp.

Record: Debka, Tikva T-100

Formation: Circle — no partners.

                Hands joined the easy way.

                All start R foot.

Music 4/4

Measures

1-4   Introduction — wait

(Yemenite backward)

A Point and Rock

	1	2	3	4		1	2	3	4
1-2	POINT ↖ (R) (no weight)	——	POINT ⇢ (R) (noweight)	—— ;		BACK ↓ R	CLOSE (beside R) L	FRONT ↑ R	—— ;
3-4	ROCK ↓ L	——	ROCK ↑ R	—— ;		ROCK ↓ L	ROCK ↑ R	TOUCH (beside R) (L) (no weight)	—— ;
5-6	POINT ↘ (L)	——	POINT ⇠ (L)	—— ;		BACK ↓ L	CLOSE (beside L) R	FRONT ↑ L	—— ;
7-8	ROCK ↓ R	——	ROCK ↑ L	—— ;		ROCK ↓ R	ROCK ↑ L	TOUCH (beside L) (R) (no weight)	—— ;

(Face center) (This is a Yemenite step)   (Face R) (This may be a slow two-step CCW)

B Yemenite

	1	2	3	4		1	2	3	4
1-2	SIDE → R	CLOSE (beside R) L	CROSS ↖ R	—— ;		STEP ↗ L	STEP ↗ R	STEP ↗ L	Pivot to face center
1-2	SIDE → R	CLOSE L	CROSS ↖ R	—— ;		STEP ↖ L	STEP ↗ R	STEP ↗ L	PIVOT;
5-6	SIDE → R	CLOSE L	CROSS ↖ R	—— ;		STEP ↗ L	STEP ↗ R	STEP ↗ L	PIVOT;
7-8	SIDE → R	CLOSE L	CROSS ↖ R	—— ;		STEP ↗ L	STEP ↗ R	STEP ↗ L	PIVOT;

Reference in Bibliography: 18 (p. 115)

MAYIM

Israeli circle dance
Means Water

Pronounced My̆-yim

This dance was first performed in a kibbutz in Israel. Since its creation it has become popular all over the world. The grapevine step which is the first figure of the dance is now called the "Mayim step" by some dance authorities.

The dance itself symbolizes the joy which the people feel when they find water in the desert land.

Records: Folkraft 1475 x 45
Folkraft 1108 (78 RPM)
Israel label 2001 — This has a double introduction

Formation: Circle.

No partners.

Joined hands are low.

Free foot — R.

Music 4/4

Measures

1-2   Introduction

Measures		(This is a Mayim step . . . .)							

Measures									
1-2		1	2	3	4	1	2	3	4
		FRONT	SIDE	BEHIND	LEAP;	FRONT	SIDE	BEHIND	LEAP;
		↖	←	↙	←	↖	←	↙	←
	A	R	L	R	L	R	L	R	L
	Mayim								
3-4		1	2	3	4	1	2	3	4
		FRONT	SIDE	BEHIND	LEAP;	FRONT	SIDE	BEHIND	LEAP;
		↖	←	↙	←	↖	←	↙	←
		R	L	R	L	R	L	R	L

Measures		(Face center)					
5		RUN	TWO	THREE	FOUR;	(Raise arms, chant "Mayim,
		↑	↑	↑	↑	mayim, mayim, mayim".)
		R	L	R	L	
6	**B**	OUT	TWO	THREE	FOUR;	(Lower arms)
	In & Out	↓	↓	↓	↓	
		R	L	R	L	
7		IN	TWO	THREE	FOUR;	(Raise arms and chant)
8		OUT	TWO	THREE	FOUR;	(Lower arms)

Measures		(Face to L)		(Face center)	
9	**C**	RUN	TWO	THREE	HOP;
	Schottische	↖	↖	↖	
		R	L	R	R

Measures									
10-11		1	2	3	4	1	2	3	4
		TOUCH	TOUCH	TOUCH	TOUCH	TOUCH	TOUCH	TOUCH	TOUCH
		ACROSS	OUT	ACROSS	OUT;	ACROSS	OUT	ACROSS	OUT;
		↗	⇢	↗	⇠	↗	⇠	↗	⇠
		(L)	(L)	(L)	(L)	(L)	(L)	(L)	(L)
	D	Hop R	Hop R	Hop R	Hop R	Hop R	Hop R	Hop R	Hop R
	Toe	1	2	3	4	1	2	3	4
12-13	**Touching**	CHANGE	OUT	ACROSS	OUT;	ACROSS	OUT	ACROSS	OUT;
		↘	(no wt) ⇢	↘	⇢	↘ (no wt)	⇢	↘	⇢
		(R)	(R)	(R)	(R)	(R)	(R)	(R)	(R)
		Hop L	Hop L	Hop L	Hop L	Hop L	Hop L	Hop L	Hop L
			(Clap)		(Clap)		(Clap)		(Clap)

References in Bibliography: 11 (p. 231), 16 (p. 295), 22 (p. 154).

MAZURKA WALTZ
German couple dance

There are many mazurkas danced all over Europe. In Germany each area has its own mazurka dance with special music.

This dance is not authentic. It was arranged by the author from typical figures found in many mazurka dances of Germany. It has no special music. Use any German mazurka or waltz music with moderate tempo.

Suggested record: Schrittwalzer or Deutsche Walz, German Folk Dances, Folkraft LP-5

Formation: Couples, woman on R.

Face CCW. Hold inside hand.

Directions are for man.

Woman uses other foot.

Free foot — Man's L, woman's R.

> **For each dance:**
>
> 1. **Say the capitalized words.**
> 2. **Do what you say**
> 3. **In the direction of the arrow**
> 4. **With the indicated foot.**

Music 3/4

Measures

<table>
<tr><td colspan="2"></td><td align="right">SEQUENCE</td></tr>
<tr><td colspan="2"></td><td align="center">A</td></tr>
<tr><td colspan="2"></td><td align="center">A</td></tr>
<tr><td colspan="2"></td><td align="center">B</td></tr>
<tr><td colspan="2"></td><td align="center">B</td></tr>
</table>

1-4   Introduction

(2 fwd waltzes like beginning of Tyrolean)

	1	2	3	1	2	3
1-2 **Fwd Waltz**	STEP	STEP	STEP;	STEP	STEP	STEP;
	↖	↑	↑	↗	↑	↑
	L	R	L	R	L	R

(Drop hands)
(Complete solo turn. Woman turns R) (Progressing in LOD)

	1	2	3	1	2	3
3-4 **Solo Turn**	STEP	HALF	TURN;	BACK	HALF	TURN;
A	↑	↰		↳		
	L	R	L	R	L	R

(Join inside hands — 2 fwd waltzes)

	1	2	3	1	2	3
5-6 **Fwd waltz**	STEP	STEP	STEP;	STEP	STEP	STEP;
	↑	↑	↑	↑	↑	↑
	L	R	L	R	L	R

(Face ptnr)
(Join 2 hands in butterfly position)

	1	2	3	1	2	3
7-8 **Butterfly**	SIDE	CLOSE	——;	NOD	——	——;
	←	(beside L)		HEAD		
	L	R				

1-8   REPEAT "A" EXACTLY

(Open position)
(3 mazurkas fwd)

	1	2	3	1	2	3
1-2 **Mazurka**	STEP	CLOSE	HOP;	STEP	CLOSE	HOP;
	↑	(behind L)		↑	(behind L)	
B	L	R	R	L	R	R

(Maneuver into closed position)
(Man's back is toward LOD.)

	1	2	3	1	2	3
3-4	STEP	CLOSE	HOP;	STEP	STEP	——;
	↑	(behind L)		(in pl)	(in pl)	
	L	R	R	L	R	

5-8 **Turning Waltz**	FOUR	WALTZ TURNS	CLOCKWISE.	Progress CCW.

1-8   REPEAT "B" EXACTLY

MISERLOU

Greek line dance

Pronounced Mízzer-loo

This dance, which uses typical Greek steps, was introduced by Mercine Nesotas and promoted by Brunhilde Dorsch. The dance was popularized by the Duquesne University dancers and has become one of the best known and one of the most popular of the Greek dances. The name of the song, Miserlou, is a girl's name.

Record: Miserlou, Columbia 10072
　　　　　　　Folkraft 1060 x 45
　　　　　Never on Sunday, United Artists 1622

Formation: Line. No partners.

Hands joined at shoulder level.

Elbows bent.

All start with R foot.

Music 4/4

Measures

1-2	Introduction — Columbia Recording
1-4	Introduction — Folkraft recording

AMERICAN VERSION

1-2	A	(Face center)				(grapevine)			
		1	2	3	4	1	2	3	4
		STEP	___	POINT	___ ;	BACK	SIDE	FRONT	SWING;
		R		(L)		L	R	L	R (no wt)

3-4	B	(Face to L) (These are slow two-steps)				(Face to L)			
		STEP - CLOSE - - STEP			___ ;	BACK - CLOSE - BACK			___ ;
		R L R				L R L			

(This may be done as a grapevine facing center, "behind, side, front")

GREEK VERSION

1-2	A	(Face center)						(Face to L)	
		1	2	3	4	1	2	3	4
		BRUSH	___	BACK	SIDE;	FRONT	___	STEP	CLOSE;
		(L)		L	R	L		R	L

3-4	B	1	2	3	4	1	2	3	4
		STEP	___	BACK	SIDE;	FRONT	___	STEP	___ ;
		R		L	R	L		(In pl) R	

```
+------------------------------+
|    SEQUENCE FOR MISERLOU      |
|              A                |
|              B                |
+------------------------------+
```

NEVER ON SUNDAY
(Miserlou combined with two variations similar to doubles and singles of Vari Hasapiko)

Variation #1

1-2	A	Dance "A" as in Miserlou

3-4	#1 Doubles	1	2	3	4	1	2	3	4
		CROSS	AND (close)	CROSS	___ ;	CROSS	AND (close)	CROSS	___ ;
		R	L	R		L	R	L	

5-6		Repeat "Doubles"
7-8	B	Dance "B" as in Miserlou

Go on to next page

Miserlou   105

Variation #2

| 1-2 | **A** | Dance "A" as in Miserlou |
| 3-4 | **#2**
Singles | |

5-6   Repeat "Singles"

7-8   **B**   Dance "B" as in Miserlou

```
┌─────────────────────────────────────────┐
│ SEQUENCE FOR NEVER ON SUNDAY             │
│      A                                   │
│      B                                   │
│                   Miserlou twice         │
│      A                                   │
│      B                                   │
│                                          │
│      A                                   │
│      Doubles                             │
│      Doubles                             │
│      B                                   │
│                                          │
│      A                                   │
│      Singles                             │
│      Singles                             │
│      B                                   │
└─────────────────────────────────────────┘
```

There are many variations.

References in Bibliography: 11 (p. 232), 13 (p. 61), 15 (p. 88), 21 (p. 49), 22 (p. 139).

NEBESKO KOLO

Serbian line dance

Pronounced Neh-béss-koe

    This dance was brought to this country by immigrants in the 1920s or 1930s.

    According to Richard Crum, authority on Balkan dancing, the name means "Heavenly" or "Celestial." He says, "There are many dances in various parts of Yugoslavia which have this name. Some are variations of this dance and others have nothing in common with it but the name. This variation is one done by Croatian and Serbian immigrants."

Record: Folk Dancer MH 1003

Formation: Line or broken circle.

                 Joined hands are low.

                 Leader is at R end.

                 Free foot — R.

> **For each dance:**
>
> 1. **Say the capitalized words.**
> 2. **Do what you say**
> 3. **In the direction of the arrow**
> 4. **With the indicated foot.**

Music 2/4

Measures   Introduction. None in music. Visualize dance one time.

	(Face to R)					
	1	&	2	1	&	2
1-2	STEP -	CLOSE -	STEP;	STEP -	CLOSE -	STEP;
	↗		↗	↗		↗
	R -	L -	R	L -	R -	L

	1		2	1	&	2
3-4	LEAP		LEAP;	STEP -	STEP -	STEP;
	↗		↗	↗	↗	↗
	R		L	R -	L -	R

A
Two-Step

	(Face to L)					
	1	&	2	1	&	2
5-6	STEP -	CLOSE -	STEP;	STEP -	CLOSE -	STEP;
	↖		↖	↖		↖
	L -	R -	L	R -	L -	R

	1		2	1	&	2
7-8	LEAP		LEAP;	STEP -	STEP -	STEP;
	↖		↖	↖	↖	↖
	L		R	L -	R -	L

B
In Place

(Two Tcherkessia Steps- - - - - - - - - - - - - -)
(Face center)

	1	2	1	2	1	2	1	2
9-12	FRONT	BACK;	BEHIND	STEP;	FRONT	BACK;	BEHIND	STEP;
	↑	↓	↓	↑	↑	↓	↓	↑
	R	L	R	L	R	L	R	L

C
Pas-de-bas

	(Pas-de-bas R)			(Pas-de-bas L)		
	1	&	2	1	&	2
13-14	STEP -	STEP -	STEP;	STEP -	STEP -	STEP;
	→	↗	↙	←	↖	↘
	R -	L -	R	L -	R -	L

	1	&	2	1	&	2
15-16	STEP -	STEP -	STEP;	STEP -	STEP -	STEP;
	→	↗	↙	←	↙	↘
	R -	L -	R	L -	R -	L

BONG
in
Music

STOMP!

(R)

(no wt)

References in Bibliography: 15 (p. 79), 20 (p. 72).

ORIJENT

Serbian line dance

Pronounced Oh-ree-yent

This means Orient and probably takes its name from the Orient Express train which passes through Serbia on its way to Istanbul from Paris. Authorities think this dance is of gypsy origin.

This dance was introduced in this country in 1957 by Richard Crum, Pittsburgh, Pennsylvania.

Mr. Crum* says that in the 1950s Orijent was one of the "most popular kolos at fairs in the villages within a radius of twenty-or-so kilometers south of Belgrade. Orijent was danced with great enthusiasm by village young people, among them workers, apprentices and students, many of whom spent part of the week in Belgrade and part at home in the village." Thus the dance could be seen in the rural areas as well as in the city.

There are many variations of this dance. Mr. Crum arranged the following steps as typical ones for recreational dancing, and the dance is included here with his permission.

Record: Du-Tam 1001 (45)

Formation: Line or open circle

Joined hands are low.

Leader at R end may lead line in circular or winding path.

If men have their own line they place hands on neighbors' shoulders.

Free foot — L.

*Richard Crum, *Viltis,* December 1968, p. 14.

Music 2/4

Measure

No Introduction

> Styling: Light footwork.
>
> Heels never touch the ground.
>
> Knees are elastic throughout.
>
> Trunk is held very erect in "A" and "C."

		1	2	1	&	2
1-2	A	TOUCH	STEP;	SIDE-BACK-SIDE;		
		(L)	L	R - L - R		

3-16 Repeat "A" seven more times (8 in all).

B

(stretch)

	1	2	1	2
1-2	STEP	CROSS;	CROSS	———;
	L	R	L	

(Straight back — one foot behind the other)

	1	2	1	2
3-4	BACK	BACK;	BACK	SHAKE;
	R	L	R	(L) (no weight)

5-16 Repeat "B" three more times (4 in all)

C

	1	2	1	&	2
1-2	STEP	STEP	STEP-STEP-STEP		
	L	R	L - R - L		
	Heels to L	Heels to R	Heels Heels Heels		
			L R L		

(When swinging heels from one side to the other keep weight on ball of foot. Ankles are close together.)

3-4 REPEAT "C" starting forward with R.

5-6 REPEAT "C" starting backward with L.

7-8 REPEAT "C" starting backward with R.

9-16 Dance all of "C" again — Forward starting L

Forward starting R

Backward starting L

Backward starting R

Reference in Bibliography: 23 (December 1968, p. 14).

OSLO WALTZ

English mixer

The dance, even though it is English and was introduced in this country by the English Country Dance Society, gets its name from a Norwegian song which is used as the accompaniment. Mary Ann Herman, the noted dance authority from Folk Dance House in New York, says that this dance is still seen in the pubs of England. It is a form of socializing with friends.

Records: Folk Dancer MH 3016

Formation: Single circle of partners.

Woman on R of man.

All hands joined.

Directions are for man. Woman uses other foot.

Free foot — Man's L, woman's R.

Music 3/4

Measures

1-8   Introduction

For each dance:

1. **Say the capitalized words.**
2. **Do what you say**
3. **In the direction of the arrow**
4. **With the indicated foot.**

		1	2	3	1	2	3	
1-2	**A**	IN	STEP	STEP;	OUT	STEP	STEP;	(Waltz balance)
	Balance	↑	(beside L)	(beside R)	↓	(beside R)	(beside L)	
		L	R	L	R	L	R	

		1	2	3			
3-4		PULL	HER	A-;	CROSS	2	3-;

(While man does waltz balance footwork, he draws his left-hand lady across in front of him over to his right side. Lady, starting R, makes a complete clockwise turn in 2 waltzes.)

5-16   Do "A" 3 more times

B

Solo

Turn

(Face lady on R — join two hands.)

	1	2	3	1	2	3	
1-2	SIDE	STEP	STEP;	SIDE	STEP	STEP;	(Waltz balance sideways)
	←	(beside L)	(beside R)	→	(beside R)	(beside L)	
	L	R	L	R	L	R	

(Drop hands)
(3-step-turn to center; Woman turns R)

	1	2	3	1	2	3
3-4	SIDE	——	HALF	HALF	——	——;
	←		TURN;	TURN;		
	L		↶ R	L		

(Join hands)

	1	2	3;	1	2	3;	
5-6	SIDE	2	3;	SIDE	2	3;	(Waltz balance sideways)
	→	(beside R)	(beside L)	←	(beside L)	(beside R)	
	R	L	R	L	R	L	

(Drop hands)
(3-step-turn out)

	1	2	3	1	2	3
7-8	SIDE	——	HALF	HALF	——	——;
	→		TURN;	TURN		
	R		↗ L	↗ R		

C

Slow

Draw

(Join both hands)

	1	2	3	1	2	3	
1-2	IN	——	CLOSE;	IN	——	——;	(Slow draw to center)
	←		(beside L)	←			
	L		R	L			

	1	2	3	1	2	3	
3-4	OUT	——	CLOSE;	OUT	——	——;	(Slow draw away from center) (To prepare for waltz turn man should maneuver himself so his back is toward LOD.)
	→		(beside R)	→			
	R		L	R			

D

Turning

Waltzes

5-8   (Closed position)

4 waltzes. Turn clockwise. Progress CCW. End with lady on man's R.

References in Bibliography: 2 (p. 69), 11 (p. 146), 18 (p. 210).

OYIN MOMO ADO

Yoruba tribe, West Nigeria

Pronounced Oh-yinn Máh-mah Ah-doo

Means "Sweet as honey."

Most African dances are improvised as the dancers dance. Dance is an important part in the life of the people because it communicates to the rest of the tribe the inner thoughts and feelings of the dancers. It is a very personal activity. Most of the body movements which are typical of African dances are too difficult for untrained people, but this dance uses only one basic step and almost no body actions. All dancers do not have to be on the same foot.

In the Bush country anyone who brings good news to the village is honored by a dance.

The author learned this dance from Odinga Lumumba, dancer and teacher of African dances, and it is included here with his permission.

Formation: A group, led by a leader, at one end of the dance ground.

A solo dancer, the bringer of good news, at the far end of the dance ground.

One basic step is repeated over and over during the <u>entire</u> dance.

	1	2	1	2
Basic step	PRESS	STEP;	PRESS	STEP;
	(in place)	↗	(in place)	↖
	R	R	L	L

Music 2/4

Measures

The Press is almost like a soft stamp with no change of weight.

The arms hang at sides, relaxed.

The number of measures given for each section of dance is approximate.

1-20	INTRODUCTION — wait, but keep the beat in place with "press, step."	
1-30	ENTRANCE — (Arms hang, relaxed)	The group, led by a leader, approaches the 'bringer of good news" who is doing the basic step at the far side of the dancing ground. She shows happiness in her face and body movements.
1-10	GREET HER —	Group raise arms to her in greeting and then lower arms. (Basic step continues.)
1-10	CIRCLE HER —	Group doing basic step follow leader to form a circle around her.
1-10	LEADER IN —	He joins her inside circle and while dancing, gently nudges her with his shoulder until she and the circle have moved into the center of the dancing ground.
1-108	CIRCLE HER — Alternate with hands and without hands	Group dances around her several times. While circling dancers shake hands toward her. (The palms are up, hands are about waist high, shake hard as though you are trying to shake water from the hands.) Circle her once without using hands — next circle, shake the hands at her, etc.

In this part of the dance, whenever the voice sings "Oyin Momo Ado," the dancers raise their hands high to the soloist.

1-12	CIRCLE STOPS —	Basic step in place.
	Honor her	Bring arms up then down: Leader starts it. (Do this when song says "Oyin Momo Ado"). Do hand shaking in place.
1-20	CIRCLE HER —	Circle moves around her again.
1-45	FINALE —	Group backs out on the last "Oyin Momo Ado."

PAIDUSHKO

Macedonian line dance

Pronounced Pie-doósh-koh. Means "limping."

    In 1969, Ms. Jan Garrity, a student at Ball State University, first introduced this dance to the author.

    This is a recreational dance which is still danced at weddings and other social gatherings. Ms. Garrity's mother, Mrs. Mary Gershanoff Garrity, danced this when she was a young girl in Macedonia. This is a most enjoyable dance because of its catchy rhythm. The dance is included here with the permission of Jan Garrity and Mary Gershanoff Garrity.

Record: Pirin Record Co. label 9608 A

          Detroit, Michigan

          Or any other Paidushko recording.

          Folk Dancer MH 45-3039

For each dance:

1. Say the capitalized words.
2. Do what you say
3. In the direction of the arrow
4. With the indicated foot.

Formation: Broken circle.

          Joined hands are low.

          Leader at R end.

          Free foot — R.

NOTE: Phrasing of the music does not match the phrasing of the dance.
        Dance to the "beat" of the music.
        Snap fingers to get the beat.

Music 5/16 COUNT AS 2/4 WITH ACCENT ON "2."
Count "2" is a tiny bit longer than count "1."

Measures

No Introduction in music. Visualize dance once through. Leader starts when the music feels right.
WHILE DANCING, EMPHASIZE THE UNDERLINED WORDS.

			(Face R)							
1-4	**4** **Skips** **To R**		1 HOP L	2 STEP; ↗ R	1 HOP R	2 STEP; ↗ L	1 HOP L	2 STEP; ↗ R	1 HOP R	2 STEP; ↗ L

			(Face center)					
5-7	**3** **Sides**		1 CROSS ↖ R	2 SIDE; ← L	1 CROSS ↖ R	2 SIDE; ← L	1 CROSS ↖ R	2 SIDE; ← L

			1	2	1	2
8-9	**2** **Backwd** **Skips**		HOP L	BACK; ↓ R	HOP R	BACK; ↓ L

			1	2
10	**1** **In Place**		FRONT ↖ R	BACK; ↘ L

```
SEQUENCE
   4
   3
   2
   1
```

Paidushko 117

PETRONELLA

English contra dance
Do not cross over

    This is an old English dance which is a favorite in the New England area of the United States. Ralph Page, a noted authority on contra dances, says this was considered a "show-off" dance because it gave the men the opportunity to show the many different ways to do the "balance." For music he also suggests "The Girl I Left Behind Me."

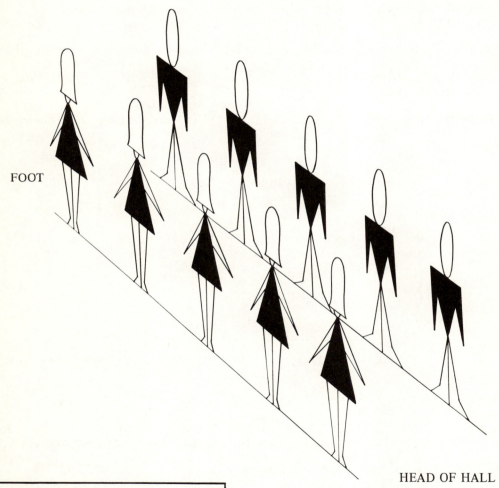

FOOT

HEAD OF HALL

For each dance:
1. Say the capitalized words.
2. Do what you say
3. In the direction of the arrow
4. With the indicated foot.

Record: Folk Dancer MH 10067

Formation: Contra, 6-8 couples. M's L side toward caller. (Head of hall)

Couples 1, 3, and 5 are active.

Do not cross over.

Free foot — R.

In contra dancing the head of the set is toward the caller. The foot of the set is away from the caller. When referring to two couples, the one closer to the head is 'above'' and the couple closer to the foot is "below." "Up" is toward the Head. "Down" is toward the foot.

The "actives" remain "actives" until they get to the foot of the set. They are "dead" for one round and then they become "inactives" and gradually work themselves up to the head of the set.

When they get to the head, they are "dead" for one round and then become "actives."

The pas de basque is a popular form of the "balance."

NOTE TO THE ACTIVES — Face your partner squarely. Pretend you are standing at "home plate" on a baseball diamond. Your partner is standing at second base. The pitcher's mound is between you and your partner. When moving from one base to another make a three-quarter turn to your R. Each time you "balance" face the pitcher's mound.

IMPORTANT: In all contra dancing, dancers must listen to the music and stay with the phrasing.

Music 4/4

Measures

1-2   Introduction

1

BALANCE

and

TURN

(Actives only)
(Balance —
pas de basque R)

1	&	2	&

LEAP-STEP-STEP _____ ,
→   ↗   ↙
R   L   R

(Balance —
pas de basque L)

3 & 4 &

LEAP-STEP-STEP _____ ;
←   ↖   ↘
L   R   L

2

(Go to first base with 2 pas de basques)

1 & 2 &   3 & 4 &

LEAP-STEP-STEP _____ ,   LEAP-STEP-STEP _____ ; (You are now on first base.)

3-4

(Face partner)
(Balance)

1 & 2   3 & 4   1 & 2   3   &   4

PAS DE BASQUE   PAS DE BASQUE;   GO TO SECOND BASE (with 2 pas de basques);

R – L – R   L – R – L

5-6

(Face partner)

1 & 2   3 & 4   1 & 2   3 & 4

PAS DE BASQUE   PAS DE BASQUE;   GO TO THIRD BASE ———— ;

7-8

1 & 2   3 & 4   1 & 2   3 & 4

PAS DE BASQUE   PAS DE BASQUE;   GO TO HOME PLATE ———— ;

Go on to next page

		(Actives only)							

| 1-2 | Down, | (Join R hands) 1 2 3 4 1 2 3 4 WALK DOWN THE INSIDE; OF THE SET - REVERSE; |

1-2 — **Down,**

(Actives only)
(Join R hands)

1	2	3	4	1	2	3	4
WALK	DOWN	THE	INSIDE;	OF	THE	SET - REVERSE;	

Up,

(woman goes R, man goes L)

3-4 — **Cast-off**

1	2	3	4	1	2	3	4
WALK	UP	THE	INSIDE;	CAST	OFF	AROUND	ONE;

(couple "1" is now below couple "2")
(couple "3" is below couple "4")

5-6 — **R and L Thru**

(With couple above)

1	2	3	4	1	2	3	4
RIGHT	AND	LEFT	THRU;	AND	A	COURTESY	TURN;

(Two ladies go across as a couple. Men also. Pass R shoulders. On courtesy turn stay side by side and turn as a unit CCW.)

7-8

1	2	3	4	1	2	3	4
RIGHT	AND	LEFT	BACK;	AND	A	COURTESY	TURN;

On repeat of the dance couple "1" will cast off around couple "4."

References in Bibliography: 9 (p. 17), 15 (p. 172).

POLKA ZU DREIEN

German dance

Pronounced Polka Tzoo Drý-enn.

Means "Polka for Three."

    This dance was introduced in the United States by Gretel and Paul Dunsing who are well known for their German folk dance research.

    The dance is especially good for people who enjoy polkas and for those who wish to practice the polka.

    This dance is arranged from the description by Richard Kraus in *Folk Dancing* and is reproduced here by permission of Gretel and Paul Dunsing.

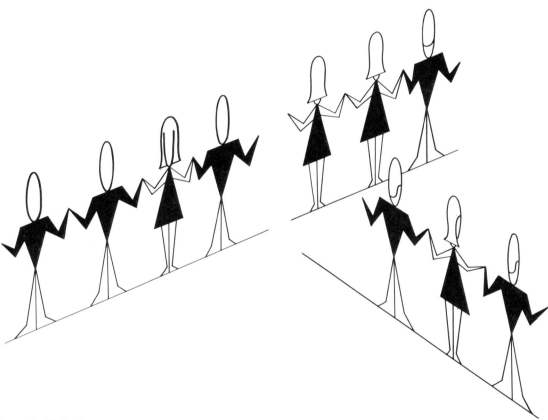

Record: Folk Dancer MH 1050

Formation: 3 or 4 side by side.

                Face counterclockwise.

                All use same foot. Start R.

                Join inside hands.

> **For each dance:**
>
> 1. **Say the capitalized words.**
> 2. **Do what you say**
> 3. **In the direction of the arrow**
> 4. **With the indicated foot.**

Music 2/4

Measures

<table>
<tr><td>1-4</td><td></td><td colspan="6">Introduction</td></tr>
</table>

(This is one Heel-toe Polka . . . .)

1-2

1	2	ah	1	&	2
HEEL	TOE	HOP;	STEP	- CLOSE -	STEP;
↑	beside L		↑		↑
(R)	(R)	L	R	- L -	R
(no weight)					

A
Heel-Toe
Polkas

3-4

1	2	ah	1	&	2
HEEL	TOE	HOP;	STEP	- CLOSE -	STEP;
↑	beside R		↑		↑
(L)	(L)	R	L	- R -	L
(no weight)					

5-6

1	2	ah	1	&	2
HEEL	TOE	HOP;	STEP	- CLOSE -	STEP;
↑	beside L		↑		↑
(R)	(R)	L	R	- L -	R

(In place) (Drop hands)
(½ turn solo to face RLOD)

7-8

1	2	1 & 2
HEEL	TOE;	STEP-STEP-STEP
↖	beside R	↶
(L)	(L)	L - R - L

1-8   REPEAT "A" in reverse line of direction. Finish facing LOD.

1-8   **B**
     Stars   Right-hand star — polkas for one phrase (8)

1-8   **R then L**   Left-hand star — polkas for one phrase (8)

| 1-8 | A | { | REPEAT "A" IN LINE OF DIRECTION' |
| 1-8 | Heel-Toe Polka | { | REPEAT "A" in reverse LOD. (Finish facing line of direction.) |

| 1-8 | C Circle (to L | { | (Each group form circle) Polka to left one phrase (8 clockwise). |
| 1-8 | then to R) | { | Polka to right one phrase (8 counterclockwise). |

Repeat dance from beginning.

1-8   Finale — there is enough music left to do "A" counterclockwise (in LOD). Do not turn at end.

More fun if dancing is more vigorous.

References in Bibliography: 2 (p. 73), 15 (p. 160).

RAKEFET

Israeli Couple Dance

Pronounced Rah-kéff-ett. Means *"daffodil"* in Hebrew.

This lovely waltz was choreographed by Raya Spivak. The beauty of the dance is enhanced if the dancers remember to keep the movement flowing at all times and use all of the music allowed for each part.

Records: "Nirkoda 2," side 2, band 6
   Produced by Hed-Arzi Ltd., Israel.

   Artza Alinu, side 2, band 1, London International TW91446.
   Israel Sings, Vanguard VRS9118, side 2, band 2.

   (This is called Harakefet. It has 4 measures of introduction and uses the sequence ABCD, ABCD, CD. Make adjustments.)

Formation: Couples — Right shoulders touching.

   Line of direction is counterclockwise. Man faces line of direction.

   Free foot — man's L, woman's R.

   Directions are for man.

   She uses other foot.

SEQUENCE
A
B
C
D
C
D

Music 3/4

Measures

1-8   Introduction — wait 8 sets of 3. (Hard to hear this, so count.)

A

Shldrs

Touch (1-4)

(Arms down; R shoulders touching)   (L shoulders touching)
(Man faces LOD-CCW)   (Man moves bkwd into LOD)
(Woman faces CW-moves bkwd)   (Woman moves fwd into LOD)
(½ turn R solo)   (½ turn L solo)

1	2	3	1	2	3		1	2	3	1	2	3
WALK	WALK	WALK;	STEP	STEP	STEP;		WALK	WALK	WALK;	STEP	STEP	STEP;
↑	↑	↑	↑	(in pl)	(in pl)		↓	↓	↓	↓	(in pl)	(in pl)
L	R	L	R	L	R		L	R	L	R	L	R

B
CW
Once
Around
Partner (5-8)

(R shoulders adjacent)   (Release man's L hand and Woman's R.
(R arm straight behind ptnrs back)   She turns L in a wide circle.)
(L arm bent behind own back.)   (Open out-finish facing ptnr)
(Join hands)   (Finish with man's back to center)

1	2	3	1	2	3		1	2	3	1	2	3
WALK	WALK	WALK;	STEP	STEP	STEP;		WALK	WALK	WALK;	STEP	STEP	STEP;
↑	↑	↑	↑	↑	↑		↑	↑	↑	↑	↑	↑
L	R	L	R	L	R		L	R	L	R	L	R

C
Step
Swing (1-4)

(Man's back <u>must</u> be to center)   (Release man's R and woman's L hand)
(Face ptnr. Both hands joined)   (She moves into LOD)

1	2	3	1	2	3	1	2	3	1	2	3
STEP	SWING	——;	STEP	SWING	——;	SHE	GOES	UNDER;	AND	PULLS	HIM;
←	↖		→	↗		(Their hands joined)			(He maneuver's		
L	(R)		R	(L)		(He steps in pl L-R-L)			himself so his		
	(no wt)			(no wt)					back is to LOD		
									while she steps		
									in place L-R-L)		

D
Waltz
Turn (5-8)

(He starts back with L foot. She starts fwd with R foot.)   (End with man's
(Closed social dance position. Four turning waltzes.)   back to center)

1	2	3	1	2	3	1	2	3	1	2	3
THEY	BOTH	TURN;	THEY	BOTH	TURN;	THEY	BOTH	TURN;	THEY	BOTH	TURN;

1-8   REPEAT "C" AND "D"

      Instead of the fourth waltz turn, she turns to her right, under their joined hands.
This turn makes it easy for them to get into the starting position of R shoulder to
R shoulder.

ROAD TO THE ISLES

Scottish couple dance

This dance was popular in Scotland during the early 1900s and can therefore be considered a modern dance. It was composed to a lively marching song and the spirited music of the pipe bands helped to popularize the dance. The music is very crisp and bright and so is the dance. Scottish dancers use very precise and exact footwork which gives a feeling of briskness to the dance.

Records: Folk Dancer MH 3003

Folkraft 1095x45

Formation: Varsovienne.

Line of direction is counterclockwise.

Same footwork for both.

Free foot — L.

For each dance:

1. Say the capitalized words.
2. Do what you say
3. In the direction of the arrow
4. With the indicated foot.

Music 2/4

Measures

1-2   Introduction — wait

		1	2	1	2	1	2
				(Grapevine . . . .)			
1-3	**A** **Point** **and**	POINT ↖ (L)	———;	BACK ↘ L	SIDE; → R	FRONT ↗ L	———;
	Grapevine	1	2	1	2	1	2
4-6		POINT ↗ (R)	———;	BACK ↙ R	SIDE; ← L	FRONT ↖ R	———;
		1	2	1	2		
7-8		POINT ↑ (L)	———;	POINT ↓ (L)	———:		

		1	2	1	2
1-2		SCHOTTISCHE ↑ L	TWO; ↑ R	THREE ↑ L	HOP; L
				(Keep hand hold) (½ turn R solo)	
		1	2	1	2
3-4	**B**	SCHOTTISCHE ↑ R	TWO; ↑ L	THREE ↑ R	HOP; ↷ R
	Schottische	(Face CW)			
		1	2	1	2
5-6		SCHOTTISCHE (In reverse line of direction) L	TWO; R	THREE L	HOP; L
		(Keep hand hold) (½ turn L solo — end facing LOD)			
		1	2	1	2
7-8		STEP ↶ R	STEP; L	STEP R	———;

On turns, do not drop hands. Each turns individually. Man stays toward center of room. Lady stays toward outside of room. It helps if the woman keeps her elbows bent and her hands in the "Hands up!" position.

The Scottish grandparents of one of the author's students said that when they did this dance in Scotland they used to do a hop before every "point" and every "grapevine."

References in Bibliography: 2 (p. 74), 11 (p. 242), 15 (p. 90), 22 (p. 115).

(THE) ROBERTS

Scottish couple dance

This dance is a simple two-step which was popular in England and Scotland in the early 1900s. It is considered an "Old-Tyme" dance of the ballroom genre.

Records: Folkraft 1161

Methodist, World of Fun M — 121

Formation: Circle of couples.

Face partner. M's back to center.

Both hands joined.

Directions are for man — woman uses other foot.

Free foot — Man's L, woman's R.

Music 2/4

Measures

One chord   Introduction

		(This is a 4-step-turn)	
		(Drop hands–progress in LOD)	
	A	(Face partner–both hands joined)	(Complete turn–woman turns R)

A
Side-Close
1-4   **and 4-Step**   { (Face partner–both hands joined) (This is a 4-step-turn) (Drop hands–progress in LOD) (Complete turn–woman turns R)
Turn

1	2	1	2	1	2	1	2
SIDE	CLOSE;	SIDE	CLOSE;	SIDE	TURN;	TURN	CROSS;
←	beside L	←	beside L	←	↶	↶	↖
L	R	L	R	L	R	L	R

1-4   Join hands and REPEAT "A" EXACTLY.

1-2

B-1
Heel-Toe   { (Open position) (Face LOD)   (This is a two-step)
Two-Step

1	2	1	&	2
HEEL	TOE;	STEP	- CLOSE -	STEP;
↑	↓	↑	↑	↑
L	L	L	- R -	L

3-4

1	2	1	&	2
HEEL	TOE;	STEP	- CLOSE -	STEP;
↑	↓	↑	↑	↑
R	R	R	- L -	R

B-2
4 Turning   { (Closed social dance position — progress in line of direction) (Body turns clockwise ½ turn after each two-step)
1-4   **Two-Steps**

1	&	2	1	&	2	1	&	2	1	&	2
SIDE-CLOSE-SIDE;			SIDE-CLOSE-SIDE;			SIDE-CLOSE-SIDE;			SIDE-CLOSE-SIDE;		
←		←	→		→	←		←	→		→
L	- R -	L	R	- L -	R	L	- R -	L	R	- L -	R

As a mixer — two ways

     A. Man progresses foward to new lady on 4-step-turn of repeat of "A."

     B. In "B-2" do only two turning two-steps and then turn woman under man's arm and she progresses forward to new man.

For each dance:

1. **Say the capitalized words.**
2. **Do what you say**
3. **In the direction of the arrow**
4. **With the indicated foot.**

References in Bibliography: 2 (p. 82), 15 (p. 142), 16 (p. 200), 22 (p. 118).

SALTY DOG RAG

U.S.A. novelty couple dance

This is one of the many simple round dances that have been composed to popular tunes. The majority of the round dances are based on the two-step or the waltz. This one is unusual in that it uses the schottische.

The basic unit is 2 schottische steps and 4 step-hops.

Record: Decca 27981

Line of direction is counterclockwise.

Formation: Promenade position.

R hand above L.

Both use same foot.

Free foot — R.

Sequence of Dance
A
A
B
B
C
C
B
B

For each dance:

1. Say the capitalized words.
2. Do what you say
3. In the direction of the arrow
4. With the indicated foot.

Music 4/4

Measures

1-8   Introduction — wait. Start dancing when singing starts.

A
To wall

(Face CCW)
(Grapevine schottische)

1-2

1	2	3	4	1	2	3	4
SIDE	BEHIND	SIDE	HOP;	SIDE	BEHIND	SIDE	HOP;
→	↘	→		←	↙	←	
R	L	R	R	L	R	L	L

3-4

1	2	3	4	1	2	3	4
STEP	HOP	STEP	HOP;	STEP	HOP	STEP	HOP;
↑		↑		↑		↑	
R	R	L	L	R	R	L	L

5-8   REPEAT "A" EXACTLY.

B
Chorus

(Grapevine schottische)
(Face partner. Join L hands)   (3-step-turn)
(Move to own R)   (Drop hands. Solo turn to own L)

1-2

SIDE	BEHIND	SIDE	HOP;	SIDE	TURN	TURN	HOP;
→	↘	→		←	↙	↙	
R	L	R	R	L	R	L	L (clap)

(Link R elbows or join R hands)

3-4

STEP	HOP	STEP	HOP;	STEP	HOP	STEP	HOP;
↗		↗		↗		↗	
R	R	L	L	R	R	L	L

(Go around partner once on step-hops.)

5-8   REPEAT "B" EXACTLY

Verse two — This is a variation — many dancers omit this.

C
Heel

(Promenade position)
(Face CCW)

1-2

1	2	3	4	1	2	3	4
				TWIST HEELS OUT	TWIST HEELS IN	TOUCH HEEL	SWING ACROSS;
HEEL	STEP beside L	HEEL	STEP; (pl)	↙ ↘	↘ ↙	↗	←··
↗		↖					
(R)	R	(L)	L	Both	Both	(R) (no wt)	(R) (in air)

3-4

1	2	3	4	1	2	3	4
STEP	HOP	STEP	HOP;	STEP	HOP	STEP	HOP;
↑		↑		↑		↑	
R	R	L	L	R	R	L	L

5-8   REPEAT "C" EXACTLY.

1-8   CHORUS two times.

SARAJEVKA KOLO

Serbian broken circle

Pronounced Sarah-yéff-kah Koe-loe

This dance was introduced in this country by Michael Herman, director of Folk Dance House in New York, and is included here with his permission.

It is similar to other kolos in that it repeats the same few figures over and over alternating the slow tempo with the fast.

Record: Folk Dancer 1002

Formation: Line or semicircle

No partners.

Joined hands are low.

Free foot — R.

For each dance:
1. **Say the capitalized words.**
2. **Do what you say**
3. **In the direction of the arrow**
4. **With the indicated foot.**

Music 4/4

Measures

1-8   Introduction — visualize the fast part two times.

A Slow

1-2

(Face to R)				(Face center)			
1	2	3	4	1	2	3	4
STEP,	_____,	STEP,	_____ ;	SIDE,	BEHIND,	SIDE,	TOUCH;
↗		↗		→	↘	→	(beside R)
R		L		R	L	R	(L)

3-4

				(Face L)		(Face center)	
1	2	3	4	1	2	3	4
SIDE,	TOUCH,	SIDE,	TOUCH;	WALK,	WALK,	SIDE,	TOUCH;
←	(beside L)	→	(beside R)	↖	↖	←	(beside L)
L	(R)	R	(L)	L	R	L	(R)

1-4   REPEAT SLOW PART EXACTLY.

B Fast

1-2

(Face to R)				(Face center)		(pas-de-basque)		
1	2	3	4	1	2	3	&	4
STEP,	HOP,	STEP,	HOP;	SIDE,	BEHIND,	SIDE-STEP-STEP;		
↗		↗		→	↘	↗	↙	
R	R	L	L	R	L	R —	L —	R

3-4

(pas-de-basque)			(pas-de-basque)			(Face L)		(Face center) (pas-de-basque)		
1	&	2	3	&	4	1	2	3	&	4
SIDE-STEP-STEP,			SIDE-STEP-STEP;			WALK,	WALK,	SIDE-STEP-STEP;		
←	↖	↘	→	↗	↙	↖	↖	←	↖	↘
L —	R —	L	R —	L —	R	L	R	L —	R —	L

1-4
1-4   DO FAST PART 3 <u>MORE</u> TIMES (4 times in all).
1-4

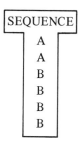

```
SEQUENCE
   A
   A
   B
   B
   B
   B
```

References in Bibliography: 18 (p. 140), 20 (p. 77).

ŠETNJA

Serbian line dance

Pronounced Chét-nee-yah.

    The name means "strolling" or "walking." Richard Crum introduced this dance in the United States in 1954, and it is included here with his permission. He say it is one of the most popular dances of central Serbia. "At a typical village dance celebration, a young man pays a musician to accompany him, then gathers his friends in a long serpentine line on his left, and leads them about the meadow doing Šetnja."

Record: Folk Dancer MH 3029

Formation: Start with one dancer.

                 Left hand on hip.

                 Others hook on.

                 Free foot — R.

For each dance:

1. Say the capitalized words.
2. Do what you say
3. In the direction of the arrow
4. With the indicated foot.

Music 4/4

Measures

1-4   Introduction

A **Slow**	(Face line of direction)							

1-2

(Face line of direction)

1	2	3	4		1	2	3	4
WALK	____	WALK	____	;	WALK	WALK	WALK	____ ;
↑		↑			↑	↑	↑	
R		L			R	L	R	

3-4

(Face center)

1	2	3	4		1	2	3	4
BACK	____	BACK	____	;	BACK	CLOSE	FRONT	____ ;
↓		↓			↓	(beside L)	↑	
L		R			L	R	L	

Slow part. L hand on hip. R hand hooked on neighbor's arm.

Repeat "A" exactly all during the slow music—first part of record (11 times in all).

B
Fast

1-2

(Face LOD)

1	2	3	4	1	2	3	4
STEP	HOP	STEP	HOP;	STEP	STEP	STEP	HOP;
↗		↗		↗	↗	↗	
R	R	L	L	R	L	R	R

Fast part

3-4

(Face center)

1	2	3	4	1	2	3	4
BACK	HOP	BACK	HOP;	BACK	CLOSE	FRONT	HOP;
↓		↓		↓	(beside L)	↑	
L	L	R	R	L	R	L	L

Joined hands held low.

Repeat "B" exactly all during the fast music—last part of record.

References in Bibliography: 2 (p. 76), 18 (p. 74), 22 (p. 200).

ST. BERNARD'S WALTZ
English couple dance

This is one of the Old-Tyme English ballroom dances which were popular in the late 1800s and early 1900s. It is lovely, smooth, and simple and is a favorite of many dancers.

Records: Folk Dancer 3019
                Folkraft 1162

Formation: Couples.

   Closed dance position.

   Man's back to center of room.

   Line of direction (LOD) is counterclockwise (CCW).

   Directions are for man. Woman does reverse.

   Free foot — Man's L, woman's R.

For each dance:

1. Say the capitalized words.
2. Do what you say
3. In the direction of the arrow
4. With the indicated foot.

Music 3/4

Measures

| 1-4 | Introduction |

A

	1	2	3	1	2	3
1-2	SIDE	____	CLOSE;	SIDE	____	CLOSE;
	←		(beside L)	←		(beside L)
	L		R	L		R

	1	2	3	1	2	3
3-4	SIDE	____	STAMP;	STAMP	____	____;
	←					
	L		(R)	(R)(no wt.		
				on R)		

	1	2	3	1	2	3
5-6	SIDE	____	CLOSE;	SIDE	____	____;
	→		(beside R)	→		
	R		L	R		

	1	2	3	1	2	3
7-8	BACK	____	____;	BACK	____	____;
	↓			↓		
	L			R		

	1	2	3	1	2	3
9-10	FORWARD	____	____;	FORWARD	____	____;
	↑			↑		
	L			R		

11-12

(Raise joined hands)
(She turns R - solo) (He maneuvers himself) (End in closed posi-
tion. His back is
SHE GOES UNDER; AND PULLS HIM; toward the line of
(Six steps for each. She starts with R) direction.)
L   R   L   R   L   R

B
TURNING
WALTZ

13-14	TURN	2	3;	TURN	2	3;
	↙			↗		
	L	R	L	R	L	R

15-16	TURN	2	3;	TURN	2	3;
	↙			↗		
	L	R	L	R	L	R

(Do four turning waltzes in closed position. The body turns clockwise while progressing counterclockwise around the room.)

End in closed position, man has his back to center of room.

References in Bibliography: 2 (p. 81), 15 (p. 96), 22 (p. 115).

STERNPOLKA

(Star Polka German Version of Doudlebska Polka)*

Pronounced Shtairn Polka

When the author attended the Workshop of Germanic Dances in Ortenberg, West Germany, in January 1973 she learned this version of Doudlebska. It is very enjoyable and gives the woman a chance to catch her breath.

A   **Polka Turns**   (Same as Doudlebska)

B   **Small Circles**   (Instead of the large circle the dancers make small circles of two, three, four or five couples. No singing)

C

MEN CLAP RHYTHM
In own little circle, men face in.

1	2;	1	2;	1	2;
CLAP	CLAP	CLAP			
THIGHS	OWN	NEIGHBOR'S	THIGHS	OWN	NEIGHBOR'S
	HANDS	HANDS			

(This gives a feeling of clapping on the off-beat)

WOMEN WALK TO STAND BEHIND A NEW MAN.

She may change circles.

* See page 36.

'S TROMMT EM BABELI

Swiss — dance for three
Means "The Dream of Babeli"

Pronounced Strahmt Emm Báh-bell-ee

This dance was introduced in the U.S.A. by Jane Farwell of Dodgeville, Wisconsin, a recognized authority in the fields of Recreation and Folk Dance, and it is included here with her permission. Miss Farwell says that this is one of the Swiss threesome dances she brought back from a week-long workshop in the mountains in 1953. The dance is from the Appenzell region of Switzerland.

Type of footwear often determines quality of footwork. In this case the schottische is heavy and close to the floor because of the heavy shoes that are worn in this section of Switzerland.

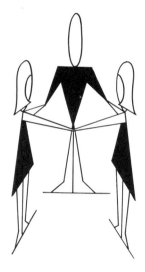

Record: Folk Dancer MH 1114

Formation: One man and two women.

Join hands in small circle.

Free foot — L.

For each dance:

1. Say the capitalized words.
2. Do what you say
3. In the direction of the arrow
4. With the indicated foot.

Music 4/4

Measures

1-4   Introduction

SCHOTTISCHE CIRCLE L

1-2 **A-1**

1	2	3	4	1	2	3	4
STEP	CLOSE	STEP	HOP;	STEP	CLOSE	STEP	HOP;
L	R	L	L	R	L	R	R

3-8   REPEAT "A-1" 3 times (8 schottisches in all)

SCHOTTISCHE CIRCLE R

1-2 **A-2**

STEP	CLOSE	STEP	HOP;	STEP	CLOSE	STEP	HOP;
L	R	L	L	R	L	R	R

3-8   REPEAT "A-2" 3 times (8 schottisches in all)

Women drop joined hands to form straight line.
Man and L woman form an arch with their joined hands. (L woman dance in place).

B

ARCHES

1-2 (R woman goes under) – (Man turns around)

STEP	HOP	STEP	HOP;	STEP	HOP	STEP	HOP;
L	L	R	R	L	L	R	R

3-4 (R woman dance in place) – (Man turns around)
(L goes under)

STEP	HOP	STEP	HOP;	STEP	HOP	STEP	HOP;
L	L	R	R	L	L	R	R

5-16   REPEAT ALL OF THE ABOVE ARCHES
<u>3 more times</u>

1-8	**C** **MILL**	{ All join R hands — like a R hand star.
		{ 8 SCHOTTISCHES

1-8   REPEAT "C" with L hands joined

1-2	**D**	{ (Man and R woman link R elbows and go around. L woman dances in place.)

D

**ELBOW
SWING**

(Man and R woman link R elbows and go around. L woman dances in place.)

1	2	3	4	1	2	3	4
STEP -	HOP,	STEP -	HOP;	STEP -	HOP,	STEP -	HOP;
↑		↑		↑		↑	

(Man and L woman link L elbows)

STEP -	HOP,	STEP -	HOP;	STEP -	HOP,	STEP -	HOP;
↑		↑		↑		↑	

1-2

3-4

5-16   REPEAT THE ELBOW LINKING
3 <u>more</u> times

     The record has enough music to do the dance through two times plus the
first figure — circle to L and to R.

     NOTE: Schottische in figure A — circle

                 Step-hop in figure B — Arches

                 Schottische in figure C — Mill

                 Step-hop in figure D — Elbow link

SWEDISH VARSOVIENNE

Swedish couple dance

Pronounced Vahr-so-vee-enń

    Many countries have varsovienne dances which use variations of the mazurka and waltz. Some people think the name Varsovienne refers to two European cities — Warsaw for the mazurka part of the dance and Vienna for the waltz part.

    This particular dance was brought to this country by various Swedish folk dance groups.

Record: Folk Dancer MH 1023

Formation: Couples in double circle.

           Woman on R of man.

           Face counterclockwise.

           Directions are for man. Woman uses other foot.

           Free foot — Man's L, woman's R.

For each dance:

1. Say the capitalized words.
2. Do what you say
3. In the direction of the arrow
4. With the indicated foot.

Music 3/4

Measures

4 chords		Introduction						

A — Cross Overs

Measures 1-2								(Lady changing to his L side. She never turns her back to him)
	1	**2**	**3**	**1**	**2**	**3**		
	STEP (in pl) L	STEP (in pl) R	STEP; (in pl) L	HEEL ↗ (R) (no wt)	———	———;		

Measures 3-4								(Lady changes over to his R side)
	1	**2**	**3**	**1**	**2**	**3**		
	STEP (in pl) R	STEP (in pl) L	STEP; (in pl) R	HEEL ↖ (L) (no wt)	———	———;		

5-8 REPEAT "A" EXACTLY.

B — Mazurkas and Cross Over

(Face LOD. Lady steps with R)

Measures 1-2								(These are two mazurkas. On count "3" L swings across R)
	1	**2**	**3**	**1**	**2**	**3**		
	STEP ↑ L	CLOSE R	HOP; R	STEP ↑ L	CLOSE R	HOP; R		

Measures 3-4								(Lady changing to his L side)
	1	**2**	**3**	**1**	**2**	**3**		
	STEP L	STEP (in place) R	STEP; L	HEEL ↗ (R) (no wt)	———	———;		

Measures 5-6								(Mazurkas)
	1	**2**	**3**	**1**	**2**	**3**		
	STEP ↑ R	CLOSE L	HOP; L	STEP ↑ R	CLOSE L	HOP; L		

Measures 7-8								(Lady changing to his R side)
	1	**2**	**3**	**1**	**2**	**3**		
	STEP R	STEP (in place) L	STEP; R	HEEL ↖ (L) (no wt)	———	———;		

C — Waltz Turns

(Closed social dance positions — man's back is toward LOD)

Turn clockwise Progress counterclockwise.

Measures 1-2						
	BACK ↙ L (on LOD)	TURN R	TURN; L	FRONT ↗ R (on LOD)	TURN L	TURN; R

Measures 3-4						
	BACK L	TURN R	TURN; L	FRONT R	TURN L	TURN; R

Measures 5-6						
	BACK L	TURN R	TURN; L	FRONT R	TURN L	TURN; R

(open position. Face LOD)

Measures 7-8						
	BACK L	TURN R	TURN; L	FRONT ↑ R	STEP (in pl) L	STEP; (in pl) R

References in Bibliography: 11 (p. 255), 12 (p. 31).

SYRTO

Greek line dance

Pronounced Seer-tóe.

The Greeks dance on any and all occasions. Dancing is an important skill in Greece and the best dancers are honored for their ability. The Syrto is the most popular of all the Greek dances. The basic step is so simple that even the poorest dancer can participate and yet the many variations give opportunities for the highly skilled dancers to show off. The leader who is at the right end of the line dances intricate variations while the line keeps the basic step or a simple variation going. Some Serbian groups call this "The Walking Dance."

The meter is 7/8 or 2/4.

Records: Rendezvous in Greece, Roulette, R 25229, Side 1, Band 2.
Greek Dance Party, Tikva LP T-131, Side A, Band 5.
Macedonka Kolo, Balkan 547 (45 RPM).
Or any Syrto recording.

Formation: Line, joined hands in "W" formation.

Hands are shoulder high.

Free foot — R.

Rhythm throughout dance is SLOW, QUICK-QUICK.

The line of direction is counterclockwise.

The BASIC SYRTO is often used as the last figure in the Karagouna dance.

Music 2/4

BASIC SYRTO

Measures

1-8   Introduction

1-4   **A**   { (Face R) (Move CCW)

1	2	1	2	1	2	1	2
STEP	——;	STEP	STEP;	STEP	——;	STEP	STEP;
↗		↗	↗	↗		↗	↗
R		L	R	L		R	L
slow		quick	quick	slow		quick	quick

5-8   **B**   { (Face center of room)

1	2	1	2	1	2	1	2
SIDE	——;	OVER	BACK;	SIDE	——;	OVER	BACK;
→		↗	↙	←		↖	↘
R		L	R	L		R	L
slow		quick	quick	slow		quick	quick

VARIATIONS

#1   **A**   (Face to L)   (Face to R)

STEP	——;	STEP	STEP;	STEP	——;	STEP	STEP;
↘		↘	↘	↗		↗	↗
R		L	R	L		R	L
slow		quick	quick	slow		quick	quick

(Moving backward in LOD)   (Moving forward in LOD)

#2   **A**   (Solo turn R)

STEP	——;	TURN	TURN;	STEP	——;	STEP	STEP;
↗		⌒		↗		↗	↗
R		L	R	L		R	L

Leader calls "Hopa" in preceding measure.

LEADER'S VARIATIONS

#3   **A**   (1 or 2 complete turns)

STEP	——;	STEP	STEP;	TURN	——;	TURN	TURN;
(Same as original "A" above)				⌒			

#4   **A**

SQUAT	——;	KICK	STEP;	STEP	——;	STEP	STEP;
		↑		(Same as original "A" above)			
		(R)	R				

#5   **B**   (One complete solo turn)

SIDE	——;	OVER	BACK;	SIDE	——;	TURN	TURN;
(Same as original "B" above)						⌒	

#6   **B**

SIDE	——;	OVER	BACK;	SIDE	——;	BEHIND	STEP;
(Same as original "B" above)				←		↙	↗
				L		R	L

References in Bibliography: 18 (p. 118), 21 (p. 48).

TO TING

Danish couple dance

Pronounced Toe Teeng

This dance was introduced in this country by the Danish Folk Dance Society of Brooklyn, New York.
The translation of To Ting is "two things" and refers to the two different kinds of music (3/4 and 2/4) and to the two different kinds of actions (waltz and walk). It is a most enjoyable dance especially if the dancers lean away from each other on the pivot turn.

Record: Folk Dancer MH 1018

Formation: Couple position.

Woman on R. Hold inside hand.

Face line of direction (CCW).

Directions are for man. Woman uses other foot.

Free foot — Man's L, woman's R.

For each dance:

1. Say the capitalized words.
2. Do what you say
3. In the direction of the arrow
4. With the indicated foot.

Music 3/4

Measures

4 chords   Introduction

	(Open waltz)			(Closing waltz)		
	1	2	3	1	2	3
	STEP	SIDE	CLOSE;	STEP	SIDE	CLOSE;
	↑	→		↑	←	
	L	R	L	R	L	R
	(turn back to partner)			(Face partner)		

1-4   **A**   **Tyrolean**   **Waltz**

	1	2	3	1	2	3
	STEP,	SIDE,	CLOSE;	STEP,	SIDE,	CLOSE;
	↑	→		↑	←	
	L	R	L	R	L	R
	(back to partner)			(Face partner)		

(In closed position. Four turning waltzes progressing LOD)

1	2	3	1	2	3
STEP,	TURN,	TURN;	STEP,	TURN,	TURN;
↙			↗		
L	R	L	R	L	R

5-8

1	2	3	1	2	3
STEP,	TURN,	TURN;	STEP,	TURN,	TURN;
↙			↗		
L	R	L	R	L	R

1-8   REPEAT "A" EXACTLY.

Music 2/4

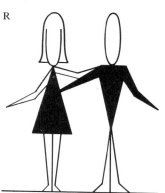

1-2   **Walk**   **and**   **Pivot**   **B**

(Move in line of direction)
(Conversation position)

1	2	1	2
WALK	TWO;	THREE	FOUR;
↑	↑	↑	↑
L	R	L	R

(Progress in line of direction)
(Shoulder waist position)

3-4   **Turn**

1	2	1	2
AROUND,	AROUND;	AROUND,	AROUND;
↙	↗	↙	↗
L	R	L	R

(During pivot turn, the right foot
steps inside between partner's two
feet. Try to progress in line of
direction. Small steps.)

5-8   REPEAT "B" EXACTLY.

A tiny pause before dance begins again.
Stand on both feet during this pause.

References in Bibliography: 11 (p. 257), 12 (p. 52), 15 (p. 93).

TOTUR
Danish mixer

Pronounced Tóe-Toor

This, like most other Danish dances, is a bright, gay dance. It is a very sociable dance, for on the grand right and left the dancers greet and speak to each new person, and they have a new partner for each repetition of the dance. Use the center of the circle for the lost and found department.

Record: Folk Dancer MH 1021

Formation: Couples in single circle.

Face center.

Woman on R of man.

Directions for "A" are man's. Woman does reverse.

Free foot — Man's L, woman's R.

Music 2/4

Measures

1-4		Introduction — wait

1-8 **Dance** ⎰ Polka to left — one phrase (8 polkas) ⎱ Done only once at beginning
1-8 **Introduction** ⎱ Polka to right — one phrase (8 polkas) ⎰ of dance and never again.

A
To Center
and Out
and Four
Turning
Polkas

1-2

(Closed social dance position)

```
  1        &       2        1       2
SIDE  -  CLOSE  -  SIDE;   CROSS   SIDE·
 ←         -       ←         ↖       ←
 L    -    R    -  L         R       L
```

This is a two-step.
Woman starts R foot. Both cross in front.

3-4

(man faces wall)

```
  1        &       2        1       2
SIDE  -  CLOSE  -  SIDE;   CROSS   SIDE;     (Both cross behind)
 →         -       →         ↘       →
 R    -    L    -  R         L       R
```

5-8   FOUR TURNING POLKAS (Body turns clockwise, progress counterclockwise around room.)

1-8   REPEAT "A" EXACTLY

1-16 **B** ⎰ GRAND RIGHT AND LEFT — two phrases—
Grand R { 16 polkas — shake partner's R hand
and L ⎱ first — men move counterclockwise. Count partner as
number "1." New partner is "15."

Repeat dance from "A" with new partner.

References in Bibliography: 2 (p. 83), 11 (p. 258), 15 (p. 137), 22 (p. 195).

TROIKA

Russian dance for three

Pronounced Tróy-kah

The name of this dance refers to the three horses hitched side by side to a sleigh. It is a very vigorous dance which is entirely different from the Russian ballroom dances such as Alexandrovska.

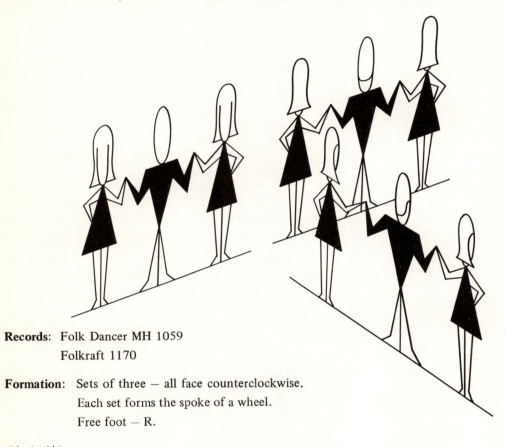

Records: Folk Dancer MH 1059

Folkraft 1170

Formation: Sets of three — all face counterclockwise.

Each set forms the spoke of a wheel.

Free foot — R.

Music 4/4

Measures

1-2		Introduction	

(Knees high like prancing horses)

Measures									
1-2 **A**		RUN ↗ R	TWO ↗ L	THREE ↗ R	FOUR; ↗ L	RUN ↖ R	TWO ↖ L	THREE ↖ R	FOUR; ↖ L
3-4 **Runs**		RUN ↑ R	TWO ↑ L	THREE ↑ R	FOUR; ↑ L	FIVE ↑ R	SIX ↑ L	SEVEN ↑ R	EIGHT; ↑ L

150

			Man and L lady make arch.				
1-2	**B** **Arches**		Right hand lady runs under arch and pulls man under (8 counts). (Other lady runs in place.) Man and R lady make arch.				
3-4			Left-hand lady goes under and pulls man under (8 counts).				

				13	14	15	16
1-4	**C** **Circle**		Circle left (12 runs)	STAMP	STAMP	STAMP	____ ;
5-8			Circle right (12 runs)	STAMP	STAMP	STAMP	____ ;

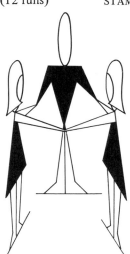

As a mixer: On final stamps, shoot the man forward under the ladies' joined hands to the next set ahead.

Vigorous and fun, especially if you pull away from each other on the circling part.

References in Bibliography: 11 (p. 259), 12 (p. 6), 15 (p. 151), 16 (p. 187), 20 (p. 58).

TSAMIKO
Greek line dance

Pronounced Chám-mee-koe.

Ms. Jan Garrity, a student at Ball State University, taught the author this dance in 1969.

At the present time this is a recreational dance. Ms. Garrity's mother, Mrs. Mary Gershanoff Garrity, had danced it often when she was a young girl in Macedonia. The dance is included here with the permission of Jan Garrity and Mary Garrity.

This is an ancient dance that symbolizes the shepherd's movements while climbing in the mountains. During the Greek war of independence it was a favorite dance of the mountain fighters.

Records: Rendevous in Greece, Roulette R 25229, Side 1, band 3

Greek Dance Party, Tikva LP T-131 Side B, band 5

Itia (side 1, band 2), Golden Songs of Greece, Near East Recording Corp. NELP 45001

Tsamikos, Folkraft LP-8 or any Tsamiko record

Formation: Broken circle.

Joined hands are head high.

For each dance:

1. Say the capitalized words.
2. Do what you say
3. In the direction of the arrow
4. With the indicated foot.

Music 3/4

NOTE: This dance does NOT use waltz rhythm.

	1-2	3
Rhythmic pattern is	SLOW	QUICK.

Measures

No introduction in music.

1-3

(Face R)　　　　(This is a two-step)　　　　　(This is a two-step)

1	2	3	&	1	2	3	&	1	2	3
STEP ____		STEP -	CLOSE;	STEP ____		STEP -	CLOSE;	STEP ____		CROSS;
↗		↗		↗		↗		↗		↗
R		L -	R	-	L	R -	L	R		L

4-6

(Face center)　　　　　　　　　　　　　　(Face center)

1	2	3	1	2	3	1	2	3
SIDE	LIFT	BEND;	STEP ____		CROSS;	SIDE	LIFT	BEND;
→	↑	↘	←		↖	←	↑	↙
R	(L)	(L)	L		R	L	(R)	(R)
	(Rise on R toe)						(Rise on L toe)	

NOTE: The phrasing of the music does not match the phrasing of the dance.

To help you remember the dance — Visualize the first step with R foot, then L foot is free to start the following:

A two - oo - step ———,
A two - oo - step ———,
Cross - side - lift - and - step ———,
Cross - side - lift - and - step ———.

TYROLEAN WALTZ

Many different countries—couple dance

Pronounced: Tie-róle-ee-an

This dance is used as one figure in many folk dances. It is also very enjoyable when it is danced without any other figures.

Record: Any moderate tempo waltz

Formation: Couples. Woman on R side.

Line of direction is counterclockwise. Both face LOD.

Free foot — Man's L, woman's R.

Directions are for man. Woman uses <u>other</u> foot.

Music 3/4

Measures

<table>
<tr><td rowspan="3" align="center">1-2
3-4</td><td rowspan="3" align="center">**A**
Open
&
Close</td><td colspan="6">(Join inside hand)</td></tr>
<tr><td colspan="3">(Turn away from partner)</td><td colspan="3">(Turn toward partner)</td></tr>
<tr>
<td>

1   2   3

</td></tr>
</table>

(Join inside hand)
(Turn away from partner)   (Turn toward partner)

1	2	3	1	2	3
FORWARD	SIDE	CLOSE;	FORWARD	SIDE	CLOSE;
↖	→		↗	←	
L	R	L	R	L	R

(Open waltz)   (Face her)

1	2	3	1	2	3
FORWARD	SIDE	CLOSE;	FORWARD	SIDE	CLOSE;
↖	→		↗	←	
L	R	L	R	L	R

On last forward waltz man should maneuver himself so his back is toward line of direction.

B Turning Waltz   (measures 5-6, 7-8)

(Closed position)

1	2	3	1	2	3
BACK	TURN	TURN;	FORWARD	TURN	TURN;
↙			↗		
L	R	L	R	L	R

1	2	3	1	2	3
BACK	TURN	TURN;	FORWARD	TURN	TURN;
↙			↗		
L	R	L	R	L	R

On turning waltz, progress counterclockwise around room, while body turns clockwise.

For each dance:

1. Say the capitalized words.
2. Do what you say
3. In the direction of the arrow
4. With the indicated foot.

UMOYA

South African dance

Pronounced You-móy-yah

Umoya means soul or spirit. The song which is in Swazi says, "I am disturbed by the spirit in the wind. I can tell that the atmosphere is not good."

The dance is an offering of appeasement to the spirit that charts the destinies of the people. It is the hope of the people that Umoya will communicate with the supreme powers in behalf of the people.

This dance, which is currently performed in the Bush areas, was taught to the author by Odinga Lumumba, dancer and teacher of African dance, and is included here with his permission.

Record: MAKEBA, Miriam Makeba, Reprise Records RS 6310, Side 1, band 1.

Formation: Any number of dancers. All face in same direction. No set formation — may stand side by side or some may stand behind in a second line.

Free foot — R.

All dancers perform the same actions but as individuals and not members of a group.

Music 2/4

Measures

1-8   Introduction

1-3	A	{	(Face forward — move straight sideways)					
			1	2	1	2	1	2
			SIDE	CLOSE;	SIDE	TOUCH;	SIDE	TOUCH;
			→		→	(beside R)	←	(beside L)
			R	L	R	(L)	L	(R)

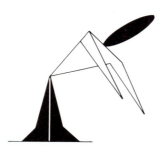

4-24

REPEAT "A" 7 <u>more</u> times (8 times in all)

Arm movements for "A" — on measures 1 and 2 the body is upright and arms reach high to right. On measure 3 the torso bends forward and the arms reach diagonally downward to L. The fingers are tight together and meet the thumb on every beat. The hand looks like a bird's beak.

The finger movements are continued <u>throughout the dance</u> no matter where the arms are or in what position the body is. The fingers meet the thumb on every beat.

1-4	B	{	(moving forward)							
			1	2	1	2	1	2	1	2
			TOUCH	STEP;	TOUCH	STEP:	TOUCH	STEP;	TOUCH	STEP;
			(flat ft)							
			↑	↑	↑	↑	↑	↑	↑	↑
			(R)	R	(L)	L	(R)	R	(L)	L

Go on to next page

5-8   REPEAT "B" <u>one</u> more time.

Arm movements for "B": Body is stiff. Both arms are parallel to each other and reach toward sky. The body twists slightly in the direction of the moving foot.

The TOUCH is not a dainty movement. It is a heavy pressing movement into the floor. Use the whole foot.

1-4

C

(Moving straight back)

1	2	1	2	1	2	1	2
DRAG	DRAG;	DRAG	DRAG;	DRAG	DRAG;	DRAG	DRAG;
R	L	R	L	R	L	R	L

Torso is bent forward so it is parallel with floor. Arms are straight pointing <u>behind</u> the body.

1-8

B

Dance "B" twice (8 touch-steps in all)

Moving straight forward — arms stiff and high.

1-8

C

Dance "C" twice (16 backward drags in all)

While dragging backward describe a circle (CW). End up about where you began but exact position or facing is not important.

```
+---------------------------------------------------+
|                    SEQUENCE                       |
|  A   Move sidewards — 8 patterns                  |
|  B   Touch-step — 8                               |
|  C   Drag back — 8 quick counts                   |
|  B   Touch-step — 8                               |
|  C   Drag back — making backward circle —         |
|      16 quick counts                              |
|                                                   |
|  Repeat dance from beginning.                     |
+---------------------------------------------------+
```

Ending   Slowly lift torso and raise arms high. Twist body to right and bend knees going down to a squatting position and touch the floor with fingers.

VARI HASAPIKO

Slow, heavy Greek line dance for men

Pronounced Vair-ee Hah-sáh-pee-koh

According to Holden and Vouras* the Slow Hasapiko was not seen until after World War II. This dance is one of the most popular dances in the waterfront taverns where bouzouki music is played. There are many variations which are used interchangeably. The leader of the short line (2-5 men) improvises the sequence as he dances. Hasapiko was originally known as the Butcher's Dance but now it is also known as the Sailor's Dance, probably because it is danced so often in the waterfront taverns. It has a marvelously mellow feeling. The author learned this dance at the Maine Folk Dance Camp in 1967.

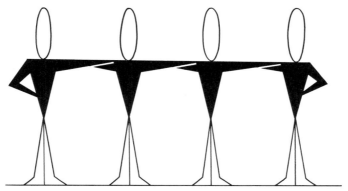

Records: Greek Folk Dances Folkraft LP-3

Hasapico, United Artists 1622

Folkraft 1462

Or any other recording of Slow Hasapiko or Vari Hasapiko. There are many.

Formation: Short lines in T formation.

Face center of room except on "walks."

Free foot – L.

For each dance:

1. **Say the capitalized words.**
2. **Do what you say**
3. **In the direction of the arrow**
4. **With the indicated foot.**

---

*Rickey Holden and Mary Vouras, *Greek Folk Dances,* (Newark, New Jersey, Folkraft Press, 1965).

Music 4/4

Measures

1   Introduction (Count 4 counts.) May be different on different recordings.

                 (Face center)

	1	2	3	4	1	2	3	4
1-2	LUNGE ↑ L	TAP ⋮ (R)	BRUSH ↷→ (R)	———;	STEP ↓ R	———	STEP ↓ L	SWING; ←·· (R) (in front of L shin bone)

                                          (Face center)

Lunge

and

	1	2	3	4	1	2	3	4
3-4	WALK ↗ R	WALK ↗ L	BACK ↓ R	SWING; (in pl) ↗(L)	LUNGE ↑ L	TAP ⋮ (R)	BRUSH ↷→ (R)	———;

Brush

	1	2	3	4	1	2	3	4
5-6	STEP ↓ R	———	STEP ↓ L	SWING; ←·· (R)	WALK ↗ R	WALK ↗ L	BACK ↓ R	SWING; ··→ (L) (in front of R shin bone)

                 (Face center)

	1	2	3	4	1	2	3	4
7-8	LUNGE ↑ L	TAP ⋮ (R)	BRUSH ↷→ (R)	———;	STEP ↓ R	———	STEP ↓ L	SWING; ←·· (R)

	1	2	3	4	1	2	3	4
1-2 **Doubles**	CROSS ↖ R	AND (close) L	CROSS ↖ R	———;	CROSS ↗ L	AND (close) R	CROSS ↗ L	———;

	1	2	3	4	1	2	3	4
3-4	CROSS ↖ R	AND (close) L	CROSS ↖ R	———;	CROSS ↗ L	AND (close) R	CROSS ↗ L	———;

	1	2	3	4	1	2	3	4
5-6	CROSS ↖ R	———	CROSS ↗ L	———;	CROSS ↖ R	———	CROSS ↗ L	———;

Singles

	1	2	3	4	1	2	3	4
7-8	STEP ↓ R	———	STEP ↓ L	SWING; ←·· (R)	WALK ↗ R	WALK ↗ L	BACK ↓ R	SWING; ··→ (L)

References in Bibliography: 13 (p. 109), 21 (p. 23)

VE DAVID

Israeli mixer

Pronounced Vay Dah-véed

   This dance was choreographed by Rivka Sturman in 1956. It is a favorite because of its simplicity and freshness. All the actions are walking steps except the last figure which is a buzz swing. The music practically tells the dancers what to do.

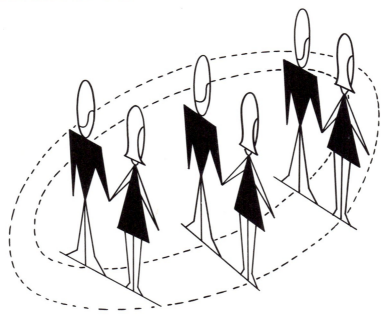

Records: Folkraft 1432

Folk Dancer MH 1155

Formation: Couples.

Double circle facing CCW.

Woman on R of man.

Both use same foot but accuracy of footwork is not important.

Free foot — R.

> **For each dance:**
>
> 1. **Say the capitalized words.**
> 2. **Do what you say**
> 3. **In the direction of the arrow**
> 4. **With the indicated foot.**

Music 4/4

Measures

1-4 Introduction

<table>
<tr><td rowspan="4">1-2</td><td rowspan="4">**Couples,
Then
Form
Circle**</td><td colspan="4">(With partner. Move CCW)</td><td colspan="4">(All hands joined in single circle)</td></tr>
<tr><td>WALK</td><td>TWO</td><td>THREE</td><td>FOUR;</td><td>BACK OUT</td><td>TWO</td><td>THREE</td><td>FOUR;</td></tr>
<tr><td>↑</td><td>↑</td><td>↑</td><td>↑</td><td>↓</td><td>↓</td><td>↓</td><td>↓</td></tr>
<tr><td>R</td><td></td><td></td><td></td><td>R</td><td></td><td></td><td></td></tr>
</table>

<table>
<tr><td rowspan="4">3-4</td><td rowspan="4">**All In**

All Out</td><td colspan="2">(All hands joined)</td><td colspan="2">(Arms come up)</td><td colspan="4">(Arms are lowered)</td></tr>
<tr><td>IN</td><td>TWO</td><td>THREE</td><td>FOUR;</td><td>OUT</td><td>TWO</td><td>THREE</td><td>FOUR;</td></tr>
<tr><td>↑</td><td>↑</td><td>↑</td><td>↑</td><td>↓</td><td>↓</td><td>↓</td><td>↓</td></tr>
<tr><td>R</td><td></td><td></td><td></td><td>R</td><td></td><td></td><td></td></tr>
</table>

<table>
<tr><td rowspan="4">5-6</td><td rowspan="4">**Ladies In**

Ladies Out</td><td colspan="4">(Women go in and out. Men clap.)</td><td colspan="4"></td></tr>
<tr><td>LADIES</td><td>TWO</td><td>THREE</td><td>FOUR;</td><td>OUT</td><td>TWO</td><td>THREE</td><td>FOUR;</td></tr>
<tr><td>↑</td><td>↑</td><td>↑</td><td>↑</td><td>↓</td><td>↓</td><td>↓</td><td>↓</td></tr>
<tr><td>R</td><td></td><td></td><td></td><td>R</td><td></td><td></td><td></td></tr>
</table>

<table>
<tr><td rowspan="4">7-8</td><td rowspan="4">**Men In**

New Partner</td><td colspan="4">(Women stand still.)</td><td colspan="4">(He moves toward next girl on right)</td></tr>
<tr><td>MEN</td><td>TWO</td><td>THREE</td><td>FOUR;</td><td>SHARP TURN</td><td>TWO</td><td>THREE</td><td>FOUR;</td></tr>
<tr><td>↑</td><td>↑</td><td>↑</td><td>↑</td><td>↗</td><td>↗</td><td>↗</td><td>↗</td></tr>
<tr><td>R</td><td></td><td></td><td></td><td>R</td><td></td><td></td><td></td></tr>
</table>

<table>
<tr><td rowspan="3">9-10</td><td rowspan="3">**Buzz**

Swing</td><td colspan="4">(With new partner, L hand high. R hips together.)</td><td colspan="4"></td></tr>
<tr><td>BUZZ</td><td>BUZZ</td><td>BUZZ</td><td>BUZZ;</td><td>BUZZ</td><td>BUZZ</td><td>BUZZ</td><td>BUZZ;</td></tr>
<tr><td>↗</td><td></td><td></td><td></td><td></td><td></td><td></td><td></td></tr>
</table>

(Beginners may use two-hand walk-around swing.)

In Buzz swing, the R foot has the weight of the body. The L foot does the pushing. With each push the L foot momentarily takes the weight. The L foot should not get ahead of the R foot.

References in Bibliography: 13 (p. 145), 15 (p. 189), 20 (p. 47).

ZEMER ATIK

Israeli Couple Dance

Pronounced Tzim-mer Ah-téek

   This dance, choreographed by Rivka Sturman, was influenced by the Chassidic sect of the Jewish people who believed in a joyous expression of faith in their God. Singing and dancing were important parts of their religious life. This very popular dance is characterized by an exalted feeling.

Records: "Debka," Tikva T-100, side B, band 3

"Nirkoda 2," Hed-Arzi Ltd., Israel, side 2, band 2
(No introduction on this recording)

Formation: Couples in a single circle. Face counterclockwise.

Woman in front of man.

Left hand on own left shoulder — palm up.

Right hand stretched forward touching neighbor's L hand.

Free foot — Right.

Music 4/4

Measures

1-4   Introduction — wait 16 counts

A
Single Circle

(Face CCW. Woman in front of man. All hands joined)
(L hand on own L shldr — palm up. R hand stretched fwd).

1	2	3	4	1	2	3	4
WALK	WALK	WALK	WALK;	STEP	BEND knee	STEP	BEND; knee
↑	↑	↑	↑	↗		↖	
R	L	R	L	R	R (Clap high)	L	L (Clap-clap high)

1-2 (measures)

3-8   Dance "A" three _more_ times.

B
Finger Snap

(Face center)

1	2	3	4	1	2	3	4
STEP	BEND knee	STEP	BEND; knee	BACK	BACK	BACK	BACK;
↗		↖		↓	↓	↓	↓
R	R (Snap fingers high)	L	L (Snap fingers high)	R (Bring	L arms	R down)	L

1-2 (measures)

3-8   Dance "B" three _more_ times. Finish side by side facing CCW. She is on his right.

C
Bow

(Woman uses other foot)
(Face CCW)
(Inside hands are joined)   (Face partner)

1	2	3	4	1	2	3	4
STEP	STEP	STEP	STEP;	SIDE	——	BEND KNEES	——;
↑	↑	↑	↑	→			
L	R	L	R	L			

1-2 (measures)

3-8   Dance "C" three _more_ times.

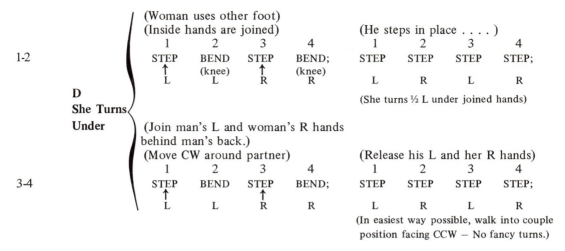

	(Woman uses other foot)				(He steps in place . . . .)			
	(Inside hands are joined)							
	1	2	3	4	1	2	3	4
1-2	STEP	BEND	STEP	BEND;	STEP	STEP	STEP	STEP;
	↑	(knee)	↑	(knee)				
	L	L	R	R	L	R	L	R

(She turns ½ L under joined hands)

D
She Turns
Under

	(Join man's L and woman's R hands				(Release his L and her R hands)			
	behind man's back.)							
	(Move CW around partner)							
	1	2	3	4	1	2	3	4
3-4	STEP	BEND	STEP	BEND;	STEP	STEP	STEP	STEP;
	↑		↑					
	L	L	R	R	L	R	L	R

(In easiest way possible, walk into couple
position facing CCW — No fancy turns.)

5-8   Repeat "D." On last measure she steps in front of him to form
single circle as in the beginning of dance.

ZIGEUNER POLKA
North German mixer
Means Gypsy Polka

Pronounced Tzig-óy-ner

This is a gay, brisk mixer which was brought to this country by Jane Farwell, the recreation specialist. Other similar versions are found in Switzerland and in South Germany. This is a fun way to change partners. The dance is included with the permission of Jane Farwell.

Records: German Folk Dances, Folkraft LP5
Folkraft 1486 x 45

Formation: Couples in closed social dance position

Line of direction is CCW

Men start L foot — women R.

Music 2/4

Measures

1-4		Introduction — wait

	A **Polka** **Turns*** **(8)**	(Closed position) (Turn clockwise — Progress counterclockwise)
1-4		POLKA TURN; POLKA TURN; POLKA TURN; POLKA TURN;
5-8		POLKA TURN; POLKA TURN; POLKA TURN; POLKA TURN;

	B **BOWS**	(Double circle — man's back to center)
1-4		1 2; 1 2; 1 2; 1 2; Bow to partner; Bow to left diagonal;
5-8		1 2; 1 2; 1 2; 1 2; Bow to right diagonal; Bow to partner;

*When teaching this dance to beginners, use the face-to-face and back-to-back polka instead of the polka turns.

1	2	1	2	1	2	1	2

(Walk to your own left — men CCW, women CW)

1-4 C
CLAPPING

1	2	1	2	1	2	1	2
CLAP,	CLAP;	CLAP,	CLAP;	CLAP,	CLAP;	CLAP,	CLAP;
PTNR'S	OWN	NEXT	OWN	NEXT	OWN	NEXT	OWN
HANDS							
(SHOUT							
"One")		("Two")		("Three")		("Four")	

5-8   Continue. Keep number "eight" for new partner.

"ONE"

NOTE: When the author attended the Workshop on Germanic Dances in 1973 in Ortenberg
Castle in Ortenberg near Offenburg, West Germany, she observed that the last figure
of this dance was different. The Germans clapped their own hands on count "1,"
partner's hands on count "2," moved to own RIGHT and continued. It is obvious
that there are many variations of this figure. At the Kentucky Dance Institute they
move LEFT. Be flexible — conform to the group with which you are dancing.

References in Bibliography: 20 (p. 50).

RECORD SOURCES

A record shop in your area will save both time and postage. The following record shops handle folk dance records. Those with the asterisk are limited to RCA (Michael Herman recordings), Folkraft, and special orders.

Eastern Area

Berliners Music Shop
154 Fourth Avenue
New York, New York 10003

Dance Record Center
1161 Broad Street
Newark, New Jersey 07114

Educational Activities, Inc.
Box 392
Freeport, New York 11520

Folk Dance House
P. O. Box 201
Flushing, L.I., New York 11352

Folk Dance Record Service
Mr. Conny Taylor
62 Fottler Avenue
Lexington, Massachusetts 02173

Folk Music International
Mr. Kenneth Spears
56-40 187th Street
Flushing, New York 11365

Folkraft Records
1161 Broad Street
Newark, New Jersey 07114

Kimbo Records
Box 55
Deal, New Jersey 07723

*Petrella's Record Shop
2014 West Darby Road
Haverton, Pennsylvania 19083

Sam Goody Records
235 West 49th Street
New York, New York 10019

Selva & Sons, Inc.
1607 Broadway
New York, New York 10019

Midwestern Area

Andy's Record Center
1614 North Pulaski Road
Chicago, Illinois 60639

Cross Trail Record Service
12130 Center Road
Bath, Michigan 48808

*Deluxe Music Square Dance Shop
4063 Milwaukee
Chicago, Illinois 60641

Leo's Advance Theatrical Company
32 West Randolph Street
Chicago, Illinois 60601

Louise Music Shop
727 Grand Avenue
St. Paul, Minnesota 55105

Makris Foreign Records Shop
813 Walnut Street
Cincinnati, Ohio 45202

Midwest Radio Company
3414 West North Avenue
Milwaukee, Wisconsin 53208

Scott Colburn Saddlery
33305 Grand River
Farmington, Michigan 48024

*Schleuning's Record Service
Route 2 Box 15
Rapid City, South Dakota 57701

Worldwide Folk Dance House
1130 North High Street
Columbus, Ohio 43201

Southern Area

Cross Trail Square Dance Center
4150 S.W. 70th Court
Miami, Florida 33155

Dance-Ranch
Carrollton Shopping Center
New Orleans, Louisiana 70118

Western Area

Aqua Record Shop
1230½ Westlake Avenue North
Seattle, Washington 98109

Cheviot Corporation
Box 34485
Los Angeles, California 90034

*Clay's Barn
P. O. Box 1863
Sierra Vista, Arizona 85635

*Decker's Records
East 3936 17th Street
Spokane, Washington 99203

Festival Folkshop
2769 West Pico
Los Angeles, CAlifornia 90006

Festival Folkshop
161 Turk Street
San Francisco, California 94102

Folklore Center
4100 University Way
Seattle, Washington 98105

Gateway Record Shop
10013 N.E. Wasco Avenue
Portland, Oregon 97216

Modern Radio
1556 Haight Street
San Francisco, California 94117

Phil Maron's Folk Shop
1531 Clay Street
Oakland, California 94612

*Recordland
4457 East Thomas Road
Phoenix, Arizona 85018

Robertson Dance Supplies
3600 — 33rd Avenue
Sacramento, California 95824

S. D. Record Roundup
8575 West Colfax
Denver, Colorado 80215

BIBLIOGRAPHY

1. Beliajus, Vytautas Finadar. *Merrily Dance.* (Delaware, Ohio: Cooperative Recreation Service, 1955.) Descriptions of 13 relatively simple dances from various countries — America, Palestine, Arabia, Germany, Poland, France, Lithuania. Price: 25 cents.

2. Czarnowski, Lucile K. *Folk Dance Teaching Cues.* (Palo Alto, California: The National Press, 1963.) A teacher's handbook. Chapters on rhythm and teaching progressions as well as good descriptions for 48 international dances.

3. Czompo, Andor and Ann I. Czompo. *Hungarian Dances.* (Cortland, New York: Quik-Print Service, 1968.) Good descriptions and some background for seventeen dances.

4. Duggan, Anne Schley; Jeanette Schlottman; and Abbie Rutledge. *Folk Dances of the British Isles.* (New York: A. S. Barnes & Co., 1949.) Good descriptions for a small number of dances. Background, piano music, beautiful format.

5. _____. *Folk Dances of European Countries.* (New York: A. S. Barnes & Co., 1949.) Descriptions of approximately 25 dances. Background. Illustrations, piano music, beautiful format.

6. _____. *Folk Dances of Scandinavia.* (New York: A. S. Barnes & Co., 1949.) Descriptions and background. Illustrations, piano music, beautiful format.

7. _____. *Folk Dances of the United States and Mexico.* (New York: A. S. Barnes & Co., 1949.) Descriptions and background for simple squares and play party games and six Mexican dances. Illustrations, piano music, beautiful format.

8. Dunsing, Gretel and Paul Dunsing. *Dance Lightly.* (Delaware, Ohio: Cooperative Recreation Service, 1946.) Descriptions for 12 German dances. Piano music. Price: 25 cents.

9. Farwell, Jane. *Folk Dances for Fun.* (Delaware, Ohio: Cooperative Recreation Service,[no date] .) Descriptions for 25 folk dances and singing games chosen especially for recreation groups. Price: 25 cents.

10. Gurzau, Elba Farabegoli. *Folk Dances, Costumes, and Customs of Italy.* (Newark, New Jersey; Folkraft Press, 1964.) Folklore, festivals, details and pictures of regional costumes. Descriptions, piano music and suggested recordings for eight dances.

11. Harris, Jane A.; Anne Pittman; and Marlys Waller. *Dance A While.* (Minneapolis, Minnesota: Burgess Publishing Company, 1968.) A teacher's handbook for several areas of dance — square, contra, round, international folk, social mixers. Background and very good description of dances. Chapters on rhythm and teaching. Excellent.

12. Herman, Michael, *Folk Dances For All.* (New York: Barnes and Noble, Inc., 1947.) Collection of 19 dances from 15 countries. Very good descriptions. Piano music. Record sources. (Out of print.)

13. Holden, Rickey, and Mary Vouras. *Greek Folk Dances.* (Newark, New Jersey: Folkraft Press, 1965.) Background and descriptions for 86 Greek folk dances. In addition to word descriptions, the dances are notated in the Romanian shorthand system.

14. Joyce, Mary, *African Heritage Dances* (Educational Activities Album, AR 36, Freeport, N. Y. 11520 © 1969.) Four African dances collected in the West Indies. The recording has three bands for each dance — instructions, music and cues, and music only. Simplifies the learning of the dances.

15. Kraus, Richard. *Folk Dancing*. (New York: The Macmillan Company, 1962.) Very clear descriptions of 110 folk dances. Useful for teachers of folk dancing in elementary and secondary schools.

16. Kulbitsky, Olga and Frank L. Kaltman. *Teachers' Dance Handbook*. (Newark, New Jersey: Bluebird Publishing Company, 1959.) A complete folk dance progression from kindergarten through the sixth grade. Descriptions very accurate and easy to follow.

17. Lawson, Joan. *European Folk Dance*. (London: Sir Isaac Pitman & Sons, 1953.) Background. The book is divided into two parts. Part one deals with origins of folk dance in general. Part two gives characteristics of folk dancing in the countries of Europe and relates these dance characteristics to the music of the country.

18. Lidster, Miriam D. and Dorothy H. Tamburini. *Folk Dance Progressions*. (Belmont, California: Wadsworth Publishing Company, Inc., 1965.) An outstanding reference. Background for four distinct areas of the world. Detailed chapters on rhythm, music, and basic steps. Accurate and easily understood directions for approximately 130 dances from all over the world.

19. Macdonald, Annette, *The Big Drum Dance of Carriacou; Its Structure and Possible Origins*. (Unpublished M.A. thesis, University of California, Berkley, 1967.) Includes descriptions of 10 dances from the "Big Drum Dance" complex. Very informative and interesting.

20. Mynatt, Constance V., and Bernard D. Kaiman. *Folk Dancing for Students and Teachers*. (Dubuque, Iowa: Wm. C. Brown Company, 1968.) Good descriptions for 65 dances from approximately 22 countries.

21. Petrides, Theodore and Elfleida Petrides. *Folk Dances of the Greeks*. (New York: Exposition Press, 1961.) Good background and detailed descriptions for 26 dances.

22. Wakefield, Eleanor Ely. *Folk Dancing in America*. (New York: J. Lowell Pratt and Company, 1966.) Descriptions of many dances from many countries showing the evolution of folk dance in America. Brief background.

23. *Viltis,* Box 1226, Denver, Colorado 80201
A folklore magazine. In addition to folklore it contains directions for a few dances in each issue. Edited by V. F. Beliajus, an outstanding authority in the areas of folkdance and folklore.